H amilton Wende grew up in Johannesburg and graduated from the University of the Witwatersrand in 1984 with a BA in English and Drama and Film. After graduating, he travelled extensively through Europe, Asia and the United States. He lived in Japan for a year, teaching English and then worked in the United States as a freelance writer and television sound recordist before returning to live in South Africa at the beginning of 1991.

His articles have appeared in *The Chicago Tribune, The New Zealand Herald, The Star, The Argus, Leadership, The Weekly Mail,* the *Vrye Weekblad* and a variety of other magazines and newspapers in South Africa and overseas.

His first novel, *Msimangu's Words,* was co-written with Windell Williams. He has also had short stories published in an American literary magazine *Buffalo Spree* and in the *Vrye Weekblad.*

A children's story he wrote, *The Quagga's Secret,* was originally published in the anthology *My Drum II.* It was also animated and broadcast on SABC-TV. Later this year it will be published as a children's picture book.

He is based in Johannesburg and has worked as a freelance television producer all over southern Africa for a number of networks including the BBC, CBC, NBC, Reuters, and SVT (Swedish TV). A BBC documentary on Rwanda, which he worked on with producer David Harrison and correspondent Fergal Keane, received the 1994 Royal Television Society's International Current Affairs Award in London.

TRUE NORTH

HAMILTON WENDE

WILLIAM WATERMAN PUBLICATIONS

Published in 1995 by William Waterman Publications
A division of William Waterman Publications (Pty) Ltd
P O Box 5091, Rivonia 2128
and
Media House Publications
P O Box 782395, Sandton 2146

First edition, first impression 1995

ISBN 1 874959 24 2

© Hamilton Wende, 1995

Cover Design by Crazy Cat Design
Typeset by Iskova Image Setting
Printed and bound by Colorgraphic, Durban

ACKNOWLEDGEMENTS

F irstly, I would like to thank the editors and journalists of *Leadership, The Star, The Vrye Weekblad,* and *The Weekly Mail* in which some of the material in this book originally appeared.

I am particularly grateful to George Alagiah and Pippa Green, who read the manuscript and offered a lot of very useful suggestions, and saved me from the embarrassment of a frightening number of clichés. I also would like to offer a special thanks to Jeremy Wightman who edited the book.

But, ultimately, my greatest debt is to the scores of fellow Africans I have met in my travels through our continent who have trusted me with their stories and from whom I have learned so much.

PREFACE

I came back to South Africa at the beginning of 1991. Nelson Mandela had been released, the Berlin Wall had fallen, the Gulf War was raging, and, through it all, Eugene Terreblanche had managed to remain unsteadily on top of his horse... it still had a long way to go, but South Africa was changing. I had been living nearly five years overseas, and I was happy to be home and keen to be working again as a journalist.

The only problem was that I didn't have many contacts anymore. A colleague of mine suggested that I give a friend of hers, Louis Du Buisson, a call.

'D'you know the Hotel Capri?' the voice on the other end of the line said.

I hesitated for a moment. 'Not really,' I replied.

'Okay, listen, you go down Louis Botha heading towards Alex. You go through Death Bend, and then past the Victory Theatre. You just keep on straight, straight, straight — past the Radium Beer Hall, past Stax, past the Doll's House, just straight. And then you come to a set of robots, where there's a parking lot on your left, and then another set of robots. You don't turn left at the first set of robots, but you sort of make a half left at the second set and then on your right you'll see the Hotel Capri just there. It's a bit complicated, but don't worry, you'll find it. I'll see you there at one for lunch, okay?'

My confusion must have communicated itself by my silence, and I got one final instruction just before the phone was put down: 'Listen, if you get lost, then you must just ask somebody for directions.'

I was back home, that much was clear.

The carpet in the lobby of the Capri Hotel was grey and dirty. It was splotched with cigarette burns that looked like large dead flies. The reception counter was made of cheap polished wood and the man standing behind it was black. Five years before, when I left South Africa, those sort of jobs were still for 'whites only'. Louis was standing in front of the counter, waiting for me. I could hardly have failed to recognise him. He'd said on the phone that he had a beard; the Athol Fugardesque figure standing in the lobby just had to be Louis.

We shook hands and he led me through the bar with its black barman and handful of midday patrons — still, in those days, all white, very late middle-aged men with thinning hair, dandruff on the shoulders of their M.O.T.H. jackets and slightly trembling, nicotine-stained fingers. We walked past the electronic games machine with its mid to late-twenties gathering of white sales reps with brushcut hairdos, premature softness around the waist, black and navy-blue polyester slacks and grey-striped neckties fastened with a full Windsor knot, but with the button of their collars undone to reveal their thick, once muscular rugby-playing necks.

Louis and I sat down at a little table in the corner and ordered Castle beer, and steak and chips. After the beer came, we talked for a while about politics, the news business and the rocky Transkei coast that I had known as a child and where he loved to go fishing. At one point, I got up to go to the toilet, and when I came back, I noticed that Louis was staring at the electronic pager I was wearing on the pocket of my jeans.

'What's the squeaker for?' he demanded.

'I do freelance television work,' I told him. 'I have to carry it in case someone needs to get hold of me urgently.'

'Hmmm,' he murmured. 'Bloody irritating things those squeakers.'

I was nervous and was trying to make the right impression, and now I was worried that I hadn't. I had done quite a lot of television work both as a sound recordist and as a fixer in South Africa and in America, but despite numerous efforts, I was still very new to the world of writing and I had not published much — a few minor articles here and there, far less, in fact, than the impression I had casually been hoping to create — and Louis was not only a seasoned journalist, but he was also a published author and, that god of gods to new writers, an editor. As an editor, he could open doors for me — or slam them resolutely shut...

Luckily, the steak and chips arrived. We ate in silence for a few moments. Finally, Louis looked at me 'So you want advice?'

'Yes,' I said. 'I do.'

He put his fork down. 'Look here,' he told me. 'You're lucky, things are changing in South Africa just at the right time for someone like you. The whole of Africa is opening up to you. If I were your age, the first thing I would do is take off that bloody squeaker, then I would put on a rucksack and go north. I would go and see Africa, and write about what I saw.'

CHAPTER 1

THE ROAD TO THE NORTH

O ur journey began before sunrise. A full moon hung in the chill black sky above the twinkling symmetry of the Johannesburg skyline; the stars were faded pinpoints of dusty light. Nine 26-wheeler Mercedes rigs were standing in the depot yard waiting to be sent to destinations all over southern Africa. The cold pre-dawn air was filled with the flicker of neon from the workshops, the smell of dust from the depot yard and diesel fumes. There was the 'clank' and 'whooosh' of the hydraulic brakes as the drivers manoeuvred their colossal machines in the narrow space between the workshops. Each one had 20 metres of truck to turn, 10 cylinders of engine capacity, 16 forward gears, 1400 litres of fuel (which would take us at least to Francistown in central Botswana) and 28 tons of load to manage.

One of the 'guys', Peter Duri, emerged out of the chaotic flurry of noise and alternating light and darkness of the depot yard. It had been arranged that I would ride with him at least as far as Malawi. After that, it all depended on how the situation was in Mozambique.

I was taking Louis' advice literally — I had a rucksack, and some other gear besides: two gas bottles and a small cooker, a bivvy tent, a pillow, a ten-litre water bottle, a fold-up mattress, a Levi jean jacket, and fifteen tins of canned food.

Peter was a short, thickset man with a half-flowing, half-clumsy gait that reminded me of the muscular self-confidence of a badger. He wore a neatly trimmed triangular beard and his head was clean-shaven because he belonged to a sect of the

Apostolic Church based in the eastern Highlands of Zimbabwe. He was wearing a sweat-stained straw trilby that was pushed back onto the crown of his head.

'You're coming with me?' he half-asked, half-said.

'Yes,' I told him. 'It's been arranged with the manager.'

'I know, they told me. What luggage do you have?'

I showed him my pile. He burst out laughing. 'You won't need all of that, I promise you!'

'Well, if you don't have room for it...' I started saying.

'Don't worry, we'll fit it in. It's just that I've never seen anyone travel with so much.' He bent down and picked up my rucksack to put it in the cab behind the seats. Just then, a thought struck him, and he straightened up in front of me. 'Have you taken your malaria pills?' he asked. 'Because the mosquitoes up there are terrible, and I know you whites have got soft skin.'

One by one, as they judged themselves ready, the huge rigs turned around in the yard and clanked and hissed and roared and disappeared into the darkness like gargantuan mechanical insects slowly lumbering into life. Peter and I were one of the last to leave the dusty compound; Boy George's 'Hare, hare krishna' blaring out on Radio Highveld into the cold of the cab, and the curve of the windscreen reflecting the stars and streetlights.

We were carrying 28 tons of soy oil bound for Blantyre in Malawi, not an exciting cargo, but then civilization, ultimately, is built on the mundane. That was the whole point of this trip, I was interested in the life of someone like Peter who travelled in Africa, not for pleasure or for curiosity, but as an ordinary job. I was grateful to Peter for having agreed to take me along, I knew before we left that I would be a burden to him — even without my luggage, and my soft skin.

We took the N12 motorway out of Johannesburg, heading west for Kimberley and the Botswana border. The radio DJ was murmuring nonsense before he finally put on 'Knights in White Satin'. The conversation between Peter and me started hesitantly. We talked of headlamps — 'too bright' Peter complained — and oil filters — 'the real secret of these

Mercedes Benz trucks'. A truck passed us in the rushing darkness of the road, headlights flicking to warn us and then, ahead of us again, and slowly creeping forward. 'Vegetables,' Peter said, in the contemptuous tone of voice that one might expect from Nigel Mansell discussing the performance of a Greyhound bus, 'a light load.'

Peter had been born in the Honde Valley in what was then eastern Rhodesia in 1955. 'My father farmed at our rural home. He had three wives and I grew up with ten brothers and five sisters. I used to look after the cattle and help with farming the maize and cotton. I finished only primary school as my father had no money for us to go further. I extended my own education by reading books and dictionaries, whatever I could find to read. My most favourite books are the dictionary and the Bible.

'I started in 1973 in Harare as a lorrymate. I had to move with the driver and work as his assistant, helping him load and offload. I got to know many places in Zimbabwe at that time. I got my licence in 1981 after failing two times, and then I became a driver myself. I joined a company in Harare which needed drivers to come to Jo'burg, and I came down to South Africa in 1988. My family lives in Harare and I try to stop on trips for a night and two days if I get permission. I do three trips a month and it's about 6000 kilometres for a round trip. I like the travelling part of my job, but there're some places I won't go: especially Soweto. I've only been as far as Baragwanath Hospital, and I won't go further in than that. I'm afraid.'

The road stretched out in front of us, a dark rushing space that needed to be filled, the white line in the centre a flickering reminder of the distance that was still to be travelled. Our headlights pierced the darkness for up to a kilometre ahead of us until the night faded first thin and grey and then into the pink and golden dawn. Lulled by the constant thrum of the engine, time began to take on a different quality. It became a rhythmic slowness that depended on 1400 litres of fuel and on the sensation of constantly moving forward past the fence-posts and thorn trees that swept constantly behind us. There would be no stopping unless we had to, but for safety's sake and to save wear and tear on the vehicles, the company strictly enforced the 80 km/h speed limit and the round tachometer on the dashboard recorded every time the speed was exceeded and, also, the length of every stop, necessary or unnecessary. The only solution was to keep moving as close to 80 km/h as one could and to brake as smoothly as possible (brake linings wear out quickly when they have to bring over 28 tons to a stop, and they cost money to replace).

The sun came up behind us as we rolled through the towns of the western Transvaal: Magaliesberg, Derby, Koster, Swartruggens, Groot Marico, and Zeerust where the earth was red and, on a thorn tree, we saw a hornbill perched, a dull bird transformed into a brilliant creature of golden, dots of scarlet and charcoal black in the creeping rays of the morning sun, and on the radio the Pet Shop Boys had become *'die Troeteldierwinkel Seuns'*.

'I was nearly hijacked here once,' Peter said, pointing to a gravel layby at the side of the road bordered by a row of gum trees with their smooth grey trunks coloured just the palest hint of mauve, and their leaves hanging limp and almost silver in the morning stillness.

'I pulled the truck over and was sleeping in the cab. I woke up in the dark when I heard one guy knocking at my door and another one at the passenger door shouting *'Vula, vula'*. I pulled the curtain aside and I saw him standing there with a gun. I pushed my coolerbox next to my door for protection. He heard me making a noise and he shouted *'Vula, vula'* even louder. I grabbed the keys off the dashboard and jumped into the driver's seat. I started the truck and pulled off blowing the hooter. Those two ran to their car and started following me. They chased me and tried to pull in front of me, to try and force me off the road, but I just kept going. I could have killed them by driving into them, and eventually they gave up and left me to drive on.'

In Africa, the morning light changes quickly; by the time we had driven through the Botswana border post, the light had lost the gentle quality of the dawn. Now the sun was bright in a blue sky and tiny mirrors of heat were already sliding off the black tarmac rolling by in front of us.

We arrived in Gaborone at mid-morning, driving through the breezeblock and jacaranda suburbs with billboards saying CASTLE — THE TASTE THAT HAS STOOD THE TEST OF TIME and bumper stickers bearing the assurance that JESUS LOVES GABORONE AND YOU. We stopped at the depot for Peter to get papers of some sort, and, more importantly, information about the road ahead from drivers coming the other way. It was my plan to travel with Peter as far as Blantyre in Malawi and, hopefully, if conditions permitted, travel with him through the Tete corridor that runs through the narrow thumb of Mozambique that separates Malawi from Zimbabwe. It was a slim hope, though, and I knew it. The company Peter worked for had banned their drivers from driving the dangerous, although much shorter and cheaper, Tete corridor. The depot manager in Blantyre could, possibly, in certain circumstances, make an exception, but it had been made clear to me that it was very unlikely that he would.

In Gaborone, my hopes of going through the Tete with Peter were dashed almost immediately. We spoke to a driver who had been through the Tete a few days before, and had narrowly missed being caught in a Renamo ambush in which six trucks were hit by rocket-propelled grenades between Zobue and Tete. 'Frelimo had three APCs to guard 200 trucks,' he told us. 'Our convoy was stretched out nearly seven kilometres along the road. The convoy kept on stopping all the time. We saw someone moving in the bush, and we decided to move on. When we got to Nyamapanda, we heard that Renamo had attacked the convoy behind us. We were just lucky, we nearly got killed — they must have just missed us.'

Peter's face was expressionless as he listened. Back on the road he told me: 'My brother is also a driver, he was going through the Tete this week. I hope he is all right.'

At midday, we crossed the Tropic of Capricorn. In the strange elastic somnolence of time on the road, it seemed already a week ago that we had left Johannesburg. The landscape around us was a wide expanse of red dust and thorn trees, freshly green from the recent rains. The afternoon heat hung in the air like a heavy, oppressive silence, and the sky was a pale watery blue, bleached almost white by the bright sun. The only things that were moving were the odd listless donkey or trio of skinny goats. For miles we would travel without even seeing a bird, and then in the distant sky you could see a kite, gliding above the treetops, occasionally giving its wings a lazy flap and then it, too, would be behind us, and the empty road in front.

The actual line of the tropic was marked by a battered sign standing in the dust at the side of the road. In a moment of time as instantaneous and as memorable as a single frame of film, we were past it, heading north.

In the hot drowsiness of the afternoon I fell into a reverie in the cab. I remembered crossing this meridian by land once before in my life, and that was on a holiday with my parents and brothers and sister in a land called 'South West Africa'. In a dusty photo album lying in a cupboard in my parents' house there is a faded colour photograph taken by my father of all of us standing in front of a similar sign due west of where Peter and I were crossing on the long road between Keetmanshoop and Windhoek.

It was 1976. The year that I first began to understand that our white world in Africa was starting to crumble. At home, it was the year of the Soweto uprising that shook our country to its very foundations. Already Mozambique and Angola had 'gone', Rhodesia's existence was just a matter of time, and my parents wanted us to see 'South West' before it, too 'went' and was consumed by the same very real chaos that was raging through the countries north of us, in Mozambique and Angola, and that was soon to intensify in Rhodesia.

My clearest memory of South West was of the rows and rows of abandoned cars parked on the docks at Walvis Bay. They had been driven down south in pathetic, ragged convoys by their desperate owners fleeing the civil war in Angola. I remember the strange foreign number plates from Portuguese Angola — a country, and a concept, that had ceased to exist — and the thick layers of dust that had collected on the paintwork of the cars that were waiting for their owners to come back and claim them.

They left an indelible impression on my mind, those rows of derelict, filthy cars, the glass and steel ghosts of abandoned lives that had come down from the North.

The North, *Die Noorde*, Those Countries North of Our Borders, Black Africa. Call it what you would, because of the travel restrictions imposed on South Africans during the forty years of the apartheid era, for the greater part of our lives most African countries remained nothing more than shapes and colours on a map for us. They existed as real nations with their attendant problems for the rest of the world, but were for us South Africans, both black and white, illusory projections of either our fears or our hopes, mythical realms located in the unexplored territory that lay somewhere on the journey between our awful past and our unimaginable future.

And then, the once-unthinkable occurred — Nelson Mandela was freed, and our real future began again. Slowly — reluctantly even, at first — restrictions were lifted on South Africans, and it became possible to travel in Africa again, after forty years of prohibition.

And southern Africa itself was in a period of its own interregnum. The post-colonial period had been generally chaotic, often disastrous, and the new wave of democratic reforms and post-Marxist economic structural reforms had yet to bring any real peace or economic benefits to most countries that had started to implement them. Cutting through this Gordian tangle of political and economic knots was southern Africa's post-Cold War challenge. It was a unique historical time. In both South Africa, and its surrounding countries, the future was struggling to be born and it was our generation who was going to be there to witness its birth.

That was really the point of this trip; and the reason why Louis' exhortation held such fascination for me. The coming process was our moment in history and I was determined to be physically present at as much of it as I possibly could.

'Ja, it's good to sleep now,' Peter said. 'You'll see when we get to Zambia you can't sleep properly because people try to steal your tyres, diesel, spanners, even the battery. So you are working double, both day and night.'

We stopped for a few hours that night on the road outside Nata, a tiny town on the edge of the Makgadikgadi pans in Botswana. We lay down on the ground under the rig in the fine white powdery dust of the pan. The moon shone overhead, bathing the countryside in a soft silvery light. On the other side of the road, a little distance away, there were some small matchbox-style houses. One of them had music blaring out of a cheap stereo system and blocks of garish yellow electric light falling out of the windows and the open doorway and stretching out over the shiny black tarmac of the road. People were sitting on benches drinking beer outside and dancing inside, and their moving, twisting shadows were long and angular on the surface of the road as they weaved back and forth across the open doorway.

Peter saw me watching the revellers (young and sexy some of them) from my bed under the truck. 'Be careful,' he growled. 'There is AIDS here, I don't want to bring you home in a coffin.'

'Don't you ever feel tempted?' I asked him.

'I'm a church man. I don't drink, smoke, or eat pork. I also don't pick up women.' He paused. 'I have six wives, four in the Honde Valley near Mutare and two in Harare. Those two are learning to knit jerseys — and I have bought knitting machines for them. The others work my field in the Honde Valley. I'm a lucky man; I don't need to think about other women. I have so many wives and I have eleven children.'

'What are their names?' I asked him.

'Chido-Anna, Crispian, Jenny, Langton, Luke, Joseph . . .' Peter hesitated. 'The others are in Harare,' he said finally.

'And their names?' I said, sitting up in my sleeping bag, scribbling in my notebook in the pale moonlight, my need for journalistic exactness unfulfilled.

'Agatha.'

There was a long silence. 'There should be four more,' I reminded him.

'Tracey, Priscilla . . . and Godfrey,' he said.

Peter woke me a few hours later. I looked at my watch in the cold darkness. It was 3:30 in the morning. I was beginning to get some sense of how hard Peter worked, and why the depot manager in Johannesburg had recommended him as their best driver. 'We have to push on, time is money,' Peter said, climbing into the cab and revving the engine, leaving me to stuff my sleeping bag in behind the seat and jump in myself.

I dozed exhaustedly in the passenger seat for an hour or so and finally woke with the jerking movement of the truck coming to a halt. A large male giraffe was wandering in a slow, long-legged gait across the road. In the bush nearby, two females were browsing on the top of a mopane tree. We had come to a stop on the top of a slight rise, and, in front of us, the sunrise was breaking tangerine and pink over the undulating plain of acacia and mopane trees. The moon still hung in the sky behind us — a slice of faded pearl in a new blue sky. We were stopped on the tarmac, waiting for the giraffe to move off the road. I wound my window down; in the cool freshness of the morning air I could smell the strong grassy mixture of cattle and circus ring — and, there, twenty metres away, four elephants were feeding in the golden, almost scarlet, glow of first light, slowly and deliberately raising their trunks to the tender leaves at the top of the tree; stripping and eating them as fussily and as imperiously as Lady Bracknell might have skinned and consumed her mandarin orange at breakfast in a sun-splotched conservatory in Oscar Wilde's Victorian England.

It was a beautiful, almost mythic, moment. A stumbling across an epiphany of Africa so serene and perfect that it was almost a vision that could exist only in a child's picture book. And yet it was heartstoppingly real, and, in retrospect, utterly terrifying in its implications for the future. In a journey of 6000 kilometres through some extremely remote African landscape, this was the only time we saw any wild animals. From that moment on, we saw not even a monkey or a small wild buck dashing in startled terror off the road in front of us.

Peter lapsed into grumpiness almost the moment we drove over the bridge across the Victoria Falls into Zambia. 'Look at these fools!' he said, sweeping his hand out in front of the steering wheel, and pointing at the camouflage-uniformed Zambian soldiers manning a light-machine gun that was trained directly onto the road we were travelling on. 'Who do they think they're going to shoot?'

Not us, it seemed. We crossed the bridge in safety and arrived at the dilapidated customs house on the edge of the town of Livingstone on the other side. It was painted an eggshell blue and every surface was covered in a layer of dust. There were more men with guns here: policemen in knee-length shorts and socks, and dirty white spats armed with old FN rifles.

Peter climbed out of the cab with a huge sheaf of papers in his hand. 'It's going to be a long wait,' he said. 'Our company won't let us bribe them.' He shook his head. 'Zambia is a fuck up,' he snarled, and wandered off to wait his turn at customs.

But the Zambians themselves were hoping for a change. Elections were only a few weeks away — the first democratic elections since Kenneth Kaunda had come to power at independence in 1964, and part of the new winds of change that were sweeping Africa in the wake of the fall of the Berlin wall. It was a fascinating time to be in Zambia, I thought, just to catch some of the feeling of excitement and optimism that was sweeping the country. In its own way, too, I thought it would be a harbinger of things to come in South Africa, and I could draw all sorts of interesting journalistic parallels. So, while Peter suffered his bribeless purgatory, I spoke to the people who wanted to sell ice lollies made of coloured, sweetened water frozen in an ordinary plastic bag; who offered to fix our tyres; to change money at black market rates — dollars or rands into kwacha; or just to talk to pass time in the stifling hot, long jobless day that promised to be the same as all the other days of the most productive years of their lives.

'Things are expensive here,' a man called Trevor told me. 'You see these trousers? They cost 1 200 kwacha, and this shirt? It costs 800. But I only earn about 1 000 kwacha a month. I want to go to Jo'burg. There are plenty jobs there — loading, offloading. I'm trying to get a visa to go to South Africa, then I can send money home to my wife.'

And after the elections, didn't he think things might change in Zambia? 'Things will be better after the election, but I still want to go to Jo'burg.'

Brian, who was 23 years old, launched almost immediately into an exhausting verbal curriculum vitae: 'I've never had a job in my life. I've made the decision now to live this life of doing odd jobs. It's better than doing nothing. I know this trucking job; I can do anything here: change tyres, fix punctures. Your wheel it is soft, I know tyres. I also know brakes. I can fix the shoes, everything. You don't have to worry if I fix your brakes — I know the job! I can help at the clearing agents — I can tip the guys, a tip here, a tip there, whatever, we can make a plan. Want to change money? I can organise that also. I don't like to steal, I like working, but the problem is, I have no job.'

Did he think things would change for the better? 'Maybe. I like Chiluba, I am a member of the MMD. I am voting for multi-party elections — the hour has come. CHILUBA! Everybody here is for Chiluba — 100%!'

He raised his hand and extended his finger and thumb outwards in a half-closed L-shape, the symbol of the MMD, the Movement for Multi-Party Democracy, supposed to represent the hands of a clock at the noonday hour — the hour has come!

But our own hour of freedom was to be considerably delayed. We had arrived at the border at 7:00 a.m., and Peter finally emerged from the crowd outside the customs house at 4:30 that afternoon. 'We were lucky,' he snorted. 'They've closed for the day now. We almost had to wait here the whole night!' He climbed in and slammed the door shut. He turned the key and revved the engine. 'Let's get out of here. Time is money!'

As we pulled out onto the road, Brian and a few of his friends waved goodbye to us, and then flashed their fingers and thumbs in the air. 'We're for the hour!' they shouted as the truck pulled away leaving them standing on the tarmac.

Peter looked at me from behind the steering wheel: 'Those people. They're so proud of their hour sign. Let's hope it does them some good.'

'Get out.'

The order was curt and the soldier issuing it was obviously drunk. There was another machine-gun post under a tree at the side of the road and the barrel was aimed in our direction. I looked at Peter, he shrugged and started opening his door, but I noticed his lips were drawn together and his eyes were hard.

'Get out!' The soldier had come round to my door. He had one hand on his AK-47 and was waving me out abruptly with his fingers on the other. I opened the door and climbed down. Peter was on the other side of the cab, talking loudly to another soldier in a language that I didn't recognise.

My soldier had bloodshot, yellowed eyes, and an AK-47 slung casually over his shoulder with the barrel pointing directly at my stomach. He looked at me with an unfocused stare.

'Passport.'

I gave it to him. He held it in his hand and looked at the picture and at then again at me. He flipped through the pages and got bored; he walked over to where Peter and the other soldier were still talking, my passport hanging half-open in his hand, the open pages ruffling in the wind.

I stood there, on the other side of the cab, intimidated and unsure of what to do. My soldier started speaking to Peter who, in turn, responded testily. The soldier said something again, more loudly, and more aggressively. The other soldier joined in with a wheedling, ironic tone, as if he were trying to make a point between friends — it was obvious that they were talking about me. Peter shook his head and continued arguing.

It occurred to me that I hardly knew Peter at all — I had met him just over 24 hours before. I was sure I knew him well enough not to worry about his honesty, but it was clear that a deal was being struck concerning me, and I was reliant on Peter and his judgement to negotiate its terms. I felt helpless, angry and not a little scared. The soldier still had my passport, and he and the other soldier and Peter were now arguing furiously. I thought of going over and asking for my passport back, but then I also thought that it was unlikely to help matters. Besides, watching Peter leaning aggressively forward, his hand movements powerful and dismissive of the soldiers' arguments, and from the determined expression on his face underneath his straw trilby, I got the very definite sense that Peter, through sheer force of will, was winning the dispute.

There was a lull in the conversation, the soldiers seemed to have given up, or, at very least, were unsure of what to say next. Peter held out his hand and the soldier gave him my passport.

'Let's go,' Peter said, to me. To the soldiers, he said nothing. I climbed in the cab first and Peter climbed in after me, slamming his door shut. He handed me my passport and started the engine. His face was screwed up tight and he didn't say anything until we were a a few hundred metres up the road.

'What was that all about?' I ventured.

'Those fools wanted you to pay them half the money you were supposed to give me for the lift.'

He turned and looked at me; he must have noticed the expression on my face.

He burst into laughter. 'Don't worry,' he said, 'I know their tricks. I've been on the road longer than they've been playing soldiers.'

Then he grew serious. 'They delayed us even more. We'll have to push on late tonight. Time is money.'

The sunset that afternoon was a crescendo of sensation. The sun sank beneath a colossal mass of billowing cumulus that glowed white, silver, purple, dove-grey underlain by a fiery orange and scarlet. A few rays of the sun broke suddenly sharp and golden through the gaps in the cloud.

The rain started falling in huge, towering cataracts on the horizon ahead of us. There was a swirl of wind that twisted the wall of elephant grass at the side of the road into strange, flattened shapes and shook the nodding, old-lady heads of the acacia trees.

And then we drove into a thundering transparent grey deluge. For a long time, Peter and I said nothing to each other. There was just the drum of the heavy rain and the feeling of safety in the cab, the wipers swaying across the windscreen chasing fat, gossamer beetles of water which bumbled frantically, back and forth, across the glass before finally disappearing into the invisible slipstream of our passage.

The downpour stopped, and the evening was filled with the complex, vital scent of the early summer rains: the red soil breathing a hint of iron, the dry yellow grass, now wet, smelling faintly of honey and fresh tobacco, and the smell of water itself, clear and sweet in the gathering darkness.

We drove on relentlessly into the night, making up for time lost at the border post and with the soldiers. There was no moon tonight, and no stars, just the heavy presence of cloud in the sky above us and the faint yellow glow of electric lights in the distance far away from the road. In the bright glare of our headlamps, there was suddenly a truck without taillights travelling at a perilous snail's pace; painted in crude, naive letters on the back: 'In GoD wE TRuSt'. Inside the cab, crackling distant Radio Metro from Jo'burg. *'Last name Simpson, First name Bart... Everybody gonna do the Bartman.'*

Finally, we stopped to sleep under streetlamps in Choma. There was a bar on either side of the street. There were young men and women and dancing and loud music spilling out of the one; in the other, I could see through the windows a large group of men dressed conservatively in jacket and tie or an open-necked shirt and slacks. I wanted a beer and some conversation, so I chose the quieter of the two and told Peter where I was going.

'We have to leave very early,' he warned. 'I'm going to sleep right now.'

'I won't be long,' I promised.

In the bar, the talk was all about the coming elections. The criticism of Kenneth Kaunda was especially bitter.

'To vote for the jeweller is repugnant to me.'

'This was once the richest country in Africa, but that old man has ruined it!'

'The non-aligned movement is just a convenient excuse for our leaders to cheat us from both sides while pretending all the time to be neutral and to be searching for the best of both worlds.'

'Socialism is dead.'

'I am an admirer of the American system.'

'And what about the British?'

'One cannot ignore entirely certain merits of the original Soviet system...' Huge cries of scorn erupted from around the room, drowning out the speaker's comment. The talk went on and on in the circuitous, bumpy way of all barroom debates. I found myself standing at the melamine bar counter talking to a young schoolteacher about my own age. 'At last,' he told me, 'we are getting our true independence.'

I finished my beer and went outside to the cab. I knocked softly on the driver's window. Nothing happened. I knocked again. Peter opened it slightly. 'Ja,' he said, peering sleepily around the edge of the door.

'It's me.'

He leaned over and opened the passenger door. I climbed in guiltily, for having been out longer than I meant to, and for waking him up knowing that he was the one who had to drive the next day. There was very little room in the cab for the two of us to sleep, but it was better than lying on the soaking wet ground outside. I crammed myself in somewhere in the semi-darkness between Peter's knees, his elbows and the gear lever. The air inside was hot and muggy and filled with the stale smell of sleep. Peter opened his window a couple of inches to let in some fresh air and we both settled down to try and get what sleep we could.

I was vaguely conscious of a burning sensation on my hands and arms, and then it felt like someone was tearing huge strips of flesh off me. I woke up to find that I was being attacked by a swarm of inch-long mosquitoes, sucking painfully at my hands and buzzing wildly around my ears. Peter was sitting up in the driver's seat, slapping his body furiously and cursing: 'Fucken' bloody mosquitoes, bloody fucken'...'

Somewhere in my rucksack I knew I had a tube of mosquito repellent. I opened the top of the rucksack and scrabbled frantically for it in the darkness amongst my bunched-up clothes. Finally, I found the plastic tube. I offered the repellent to Peter first. He looked at it suspiciously. 'Put some on,' I told him. He opened it, and the perfumed, chemical smell of the repellent filled the cab. He smeared the stick on his hands, his arms and on the edge of his ears and handed it back to me. It was an amazing compound, the moment I rubbed it on, the mosquitoes that had been harassing me so mercilessly simply disappeared. Peter was also impressed. 'It's good stuff that. It really does keep the mosquitoes away,' he said, and settled back into the position he had been lying in before.

I rearranged myself into my former semi-comfortable position around the gear lever and Peter's body.

'*So, then,*' I couldn't help thinking to myself, '*you whites have got soft skin?*'

But in the muggy darkness of the cab there was only the steady rattle of Peter snoring.

Manenekera — if you go you'll never come back. It's what the truckers call the high, tortuous pass that winds through the Muchinga escarpment in south-eastern Zambia. It is a place of extraordinary beauty. At the top of the pass one can look in any direction: north, east, south, west for miles and see endless rumpled vistas of African hills and valleys extending into the dusty horizon. From there, steep, soaring slopes lead down into a green valley with a silver, meandering ribbon of a river reflecting the late afternoon sun in the distance far below.

It is also a place of death. The rusting hulks of trucks and cars litter the steep embankments, some of them are nothing more than tiny angular specks hundreds of metres down in the valley. Peter changed down into lowest gear and crawled carefully up the gradient at 15 kilometres per hour. It was this sort of caution that made him the company's most trusted driver, and made me grateful I was travelling with him, and not with someone else. About halfway up the pass, we came across a crowd of people standing at the edge of the tarmac. A large articulated rig had plunged off the edge of the road and lay in a small depression of earth — a mangled heap of twisted metal, slashed rubber and shattered glass. Miraculously, the truck was caught in this shallow basin of red earth and did not go plunging and rolling down the two-three-four hundred metre slope that lay beyond. A man's shoe and a woman's torn sundress were lying on the ground just near the wreckage. No one was killed, but five people were taken to hospital, a soldier standing guard over the valuable remains of the rig told us.

Peter went over to where the wheels were standing up above the wreckage. He put his hand on one of the wheels and pushed; it spun freely. 'His brakes failed,' Peter said. Normally, if the hydraulics are cut, the brakes should lock automatically. 'It wasn't his fault.'

It was late afternoon by the time we reached the top of the pass. The air was cool in its mountaintop stillness; all along the black-and-white painted barrier rails, the names of people who have died on the slopes here were scratched in crude letters: *C. Manarara, Tommy, Randall 6.3.1984, END HERE Mwamainda.*

At the top of the pass, the road began to flatten out onto a plateau. In the distance, another truck, heading west, appeared. As we grew closer, Peter changed down to slow his vehicle in anticipation of passing the other vehicle on the narrow road. We came around a bend, and, in a thundering flash, the other truck was past us.

'That's my brother!' Peter shouted out, and in a clanking swirl of brakes, gears and dust we pulled over onto the edge of the road. Peter's brother had seen him too, and had stopped a few metres down the road on the other side. They both climbed out, and walked rapidly down the middle of the road towards each other. The two of them greeted one another loudly, and excitedly. There was the triple African handshake and a brief hug. Peter's brother was a thinner, taller version of himself, with the same shaven head (no trilby), and neat, triangular beard. The two of them were talking in Shona, which I cannot understand, but it was clear that the subject was the recent ambush in the Tete corridor. Peter's brother did most of the talking, and Peter grew more and more serious, nodding his head from time to time, and making muted exclamations of anger and surprise.

I stood a little way back from the two of them, not wanting to interfere in their reunion. I knew Peter, although he hadn't said much, had been worried about his brother after hearing about the ambush. After a few moments Peter called me over and introduced me to his brother, also Peter, and in reality, a half-brother which explained why they shared the same name. But in Africa family ties go deep, and Peter and his brother were filled with quiet joy at being able to meet like this, so unexpectedly. The three of us stood there in the cooling early-evening air, the smell of nearby cooking fires from a group of huts nearby, a swirl of flying ants climbing into the air above the thorn trees, talking of what had happened, over a thousand miles away in the remote bush of Mozambique. Peter's brother was there when the convoy got hit. Four 7-ton trucks were hit with rocket grenades, and three people were killed, hacked to death with bayonets and machetes. 'But I was lucky,' Peter's brother said. 'I was at the back of the convoy and the *matsangas* [Renamo] hit the middle of it. They left us alone this time.'

We spent only a few minutes talking together at the side of the road, perhaps ten at most, and then both brothers felt the urge to get moving again. We said goodbye; and then went back to our trucks, with both Peter and his brother climbing in and scarcely looking back, concentrating on the journey ahead.

Peter closed his door and shoved his hand under the steering wheel to start the engine. 'We've got to get moving,' he began. 'Time...'

'...is money,' I said.

We both laughed. 'I see you are learning something about the trucking business.'

We reached Blantyre, Malawi, at mid-morning the following day. It was Peter's final destination before he was to set off to Johannesburg through Zimbabwe. I wanted somehow to try and get to Mozambique to cover something of the ongoing civil war there, so it was the end of our journey together. We stopped off at the depot, and Peter took me inside the workshop and up a worn wooden staircase to where the depot manager, Charlie Richardson, was working behind a grey steel desk piled high with orders, customs forms, carnet certificates, and countless other documents needed for cross-border trucking.

He looked up from his paperwork when we entered the room. He had red hair, glasses, and a brusque manner that hid the generousness that lay beneath.

'Howzit Peter,' he said. 'Had a good trip?'

'Ja, Charlie, not bad.' I got the sense that it was something of an unconscious ritual greeting between the two of them. For a moment there was a stilted silence, until Charlie looked over in my direction, and began a friendly interrogation:

'So you're the journalist from South, hey? I heard from Jo'burg you were coming. How was the trip? A bit of a shock, I suppose, roughing it like that?'

A lot of questions. I certainly couldn't answer them all at once. I said something about the journey being 'okay'.

'Well, listen, get your stuff out of Peter's truck and come back up here. You can stay at my place tonight, and then we'll discuss what your next move is.'

Peter and I went downstairs together and walked outside to where his truck was parked in the hot, mid-morning sunshine. I climbed up into the cab and started taking my things out. Peter stood on the ground and I handed them to him, and he put them in a neat pile on the ground next to him.

I climbed down from the cab and put my hand out. 'Thanks,' I said. 'For everything.' We shook hands. A triple handshake, down-up-down again, African-style.

'It was good to travel with you,' Peter said. 'Watch out for those matsangas in Mozambique.' The two of us stood in silence for a few moments, neither of us sure what to say next.

'Well, Peter said finally. 'I must get going. Time...' he didn't need to finish the sentence.

And so my first journey ended at sunset, on the balcony of the Blantyre Club that evening. Sitting there with Charlie and some other men on the wire chairs with chipped paint, and sharp curling points, drinking the locally brewed Carlsberg beer, I entered a different world from the one I had been living in so intensely for the past few days. It was a small, rarified world surrounded by shady trees and rolling lawns that seemed scarcely real after the journey I had just made. It was a tiny white, colonial, world deep in the middle of Africa with a few black members who had joined the club.

It seemed ironic that such a club still existed in post-colonial Africa. Thirty years into independence and the worlds of white and black still ran on parallel, but largely separate, lines. The one area where they did come together was at work, and on the common threat that the violence in Mozambique posed to their livelihoods. The talk here, among Charlie and his friends, bore a remarkable similarity to the conversation among Peter and his — the discussion was all about last week's ambush:

'It happened at a bridge 57 kilometres out of Zobue, they were almost safely back in Malawi...'

'They let the first 12 vehicles through and then Renamo hit them at about 1:30 in the afternoon...'

'The escort vehicles were at the back of the convoy...'

'One of the escort vehicles tried to get back to protect the convoy and a group of Renamo hit them with an RPG...'

'Seven people were killed and nine wounded in that ambush...'

'It was unusual, no one was chopped by pangas, they were all hit by bullets...'

Finally, the story had been told, all the snippets of information had been exchanged. The others drifted away, leaving me and Charlie sitting alone. I ordered another round of drinks.

'Why do you want to go down that road?' Charlie asked.

The eternal question. 'Well,' I mumbled, 'it's a good story. The closest you can get to the war in Mozambique.'

Charlie looked at me. 'When Renamo does attack pandemonium breaks out. The vehicles smash into one another. Some unhitch and drive off into the bush to try and escape, others do U-turns and get caught in the firestorm. It's bloody dangerous.'

'What's the best thing to do if you are hit.'

Charlie sat back and laughed. 'The best thing to do is to try and get the fuck out of there!'

And failing that?

'What the drivers have been taught to do is to climb under the horse and lie on the diff — it's not the coolest place in the world, but you must lie on top of the diff. It's the best hiding place, and also, if you lie underneath and the tyres are shot out in crossfire and the cab collapses you'll be crushed between the diff and the tarmac.'

'There is,' I simply had to ask, 'enough room for two?'

Charlie smiled. 'Perhaps.'

CHAPTER 2

MOZAMBIQUE
PART 1 – HELL'S FORGOTTEN HIGHWAY

O ver the years 1991–1994, I found myself going to Mozambique quite often. The impressions I formed of the country and of the war as it ground, slowly, exhaustedly, to an end, were sporadic and took time to mould into some sort of coherent mosaic.

Those years were a slow, but relentless turning point in Mozambican history. At the end of the 1980s, almost overnight, the familiar certainties of the post-colonial era and the Cold War had disappeared. The brutal destabilisation policies of Rhodesia and apartheid South Africa had been replaced by growing regional cooperation. Failed Marxist ideologies had been driven out by new market realities; the ravages of war were slowly being swopped for the pillage of tourists, hungry for prawns, cold beer and sunshine. All the while, in Mozambique itself over 500 000 people had died either as a direct result of the fighting, or because of starvation, and there were over three million refugees and internally displaced people who had fled the war.

The devastation wrought by the hasty pull-out of the Portuguese colonial masters in 1974 followed by nearly twenty years of civil war and cyclical droughts had reduced Mozambique to absolute penury, and by 1990 a World Bank report named Mozambique as the poorest country in the world.

Mozambique was, and is, filled with ironies and contra-dictions that defeat even the most ardent moralists and the most conscientious political theorists. There was Maputo, with its solid Frelimo support but then, too, there was Beira with its hidden, but large, Renamo support; there was the drought and the unspeakable poverty, but there were also the luxury tourist lodges and the glittering Polana Hotel; there was Christian and Muslim; there was black and white; Indian and African; there was expat aid worker and resentful citizen; there were the cities, with their broken veneer of chic Afro-Latin culture, and there were the deep rural areas where people lived as they had since the beginning of time and believed what the sangomas told them, that they could perform a magic that would turn Renamo's bullets to water...

There were as many Mozambiques as there are ways of seeing.

1

I am awakened by a loud banging on my door. It is still dark outside, but there is the sound of birds in the darkness that lets me know dawn is not far off.

The knock again. It is the young boy who showed me to my tiny, filthy room the previous evening, after Charlie had dropped me off.

'Wake up, please,' he says from behind the loose collection of wooden planks that make up the door. 'It is time to leave, or you will miss your lift.'

I am happy to be leaving. My night at the Mwanza Rest House (comfortable rooms and clean beds) has been one of the worst I have ever experienced in my life. The room was cheap enough at 4 Malawian kwacha — the equivalent then of about one American dollar, but there had been no light of any kind and in the darkness, I had heard the rustling of insects all around me. Once, I had struck a match. In the wavering light it threw, I saw at least three two-inch long cockroaches staring at me from the wall opposite the bed. Hurriedly, I blew it out and hoped that exhaustion from the previous day's travelling would allow me to get some sleep.

I slept fitfully, and the coolness of the morning has come as a welcome relief from the spasmodic ugliness of my dreams

and the choking squalor of the room. I pick up my knapsack
and go outside. The light is just beginning to gather in a grey
haze above the trees. I walk down to the petrol station where,
the night before, I agreed to meet Laxton, the Zimbabwean
truck driver who is to give me a lift from Zobue, at the
Malawian border, through the Tete corridor to Nyamapanda
in Zimbabwe.

We had settled on a price of one hundred Zimbabwean
dollars for the trip. He said he would meet me at the petrol
station the next morning. He agreed to be paid half up front
and half at the end of the trip. We smiled at each other and
shook hands. 'Bring some Malawian water and food,' he told
me. 'It is too easy to get sick in Mozambique.' Then he went
off to stay at his girlfriend's house in town, leaving me to seek
alternative sleeping arrangements on my own.

The petrol station is surrounded by a clean, well-swept
gravel parking area. Separating the premises from the road is
a flower bed, filled with colour. Behind the office is a
vegetable garden with squash, spinach, tomatoes and two
stumpy paw-paw trees. This is much more like the Malawi I
know than the Mwanza Rest House. My spirits are lifted
slightly by seeing this order and cleanliness around me. I sit
down to wait for Laxton to arrive.

Dawn is beginning to break through the acacia trees at the
edge of the road. The horizon is pink and orange; the pale,
leftover moon a crumbling, delicately veined seashell in a
wash of violet. A rooster starts screeching from a cluster of
huts a few hundred metres away, their conical roofs a dark,
triangular silhouette against the dawn light. Somewhere,
further away, there is the clutter of pans and the low murmur
of a woman's voice. Daybreak in Africa is cool and forgiving.
It hints of abundance and of peace — of the Eden that
Westerners imagine Meryl Streep and Robert Redford to have
wandered serenely through in *Out of Africa*. Dawn hides the
poverty and the disease and the conflict that underlies so
much of the continent. And yet, it is not all pretty lies — the
light is beautiful and streaked with amber, the trees are filled
with birds that are singing and the half-forgotten moon does

hang in the dark sky until it fades graciously into the grey morning light.

In the distance, I can hear the rumble of an engine. I get up and look down the road. I can see a pair of headlights. The sound of the engine grows louder. The headlights grow brighter. There is the hissing, clanking sound of airbrakes being applied and the truck comes to a halt in front of me. It is Laxton.

I climb awkwardly into the cab and sling my rucksack on the makeshift bed behind the seats. Laxton engages gear and we set off down the road.

'How did you sleep?' he asks politely.

I tell him about the Mwanza Rest House. His eyes widen in amused horror. 'You stayed *there*.' He cannot believe his ears. 'But it is only for prostitutes and drunks.' He shakes his head and laughs. 'You were lucky not to be robbed.'

2

The narrow strip of road that runs between Zobue in Mozambique and Nyamapanda in Zimbabwe through the Zambezi Valley is known as the Tete corridor. For cargo travelling between Malawi, Zambia, Zimbabwe, Tanzania, northern Mozambique, South Africa it is often the cheapest and shortest route. In former times it was a bustling trucking route — one of the lifelines of southern Africa, and now again, with the coming of peace, the traffic has started flowing.

But at the height of the Mozambican civil war, when Laxton and I travelled through it, it was one of the most dangerous stretches of road anywhere in the world. Renamo rebels attacked convoys of trucks going through on a regular basis. Actual figures were hard to come by. The situation was too confused and dangerous for any organisation to monitor it accurately. The only real source of information was from the truckers who drove the route, but that was mostly rumour and stories that had been passed by word of mouth from driver to driver, like Peter and his brother.

One thing is certain: at the height of the war, there were plenty of attacks and the killings in the Tete corridor; at least twice a month convoys were attacked, often more frequently. Meetings between Renamo and Frelimo were held, and the attacks went on. A peace accord was signed in Rome, and the attacks went on. The Zimbabwean army was withdrawn to comply with the agreement, and the attacks went on... there was little or no press coverage of them — it was just another local, Third-World war.

3

The collection point for the convoy is 20 kilometres or so inside the Mozambique border from Zobue, just outside a Frelimo army outpost. When we arrive, a few officers are lounging on the side of the road in the shade of a low-walled rondavel; while from the bush around us, a number of ragtag teenage soldiers emerge dressed in a motley array of faded, sometimes ripped camouflage fatigues, T-shirts and odd shoes: slip-slops held together with wire, old takkies, worn-out combat boots. All of the soldiers are armed with AK-47s and they go from truck to truck, begging for anything they can get from the drivers.

There is no hostility or pushiness about them, (certainly towards me, the lone white person there). It may be different for the black drivers, Laxton is very uneasy when they are around. One of them points at my hiking boots and then taps his own chest. I give him two Malawian Life cigarettes which seems to satisfy him.

The cigarettes bring over a trio of soldiers who come up to the cab to beg them from me. None of them can be older than fifteen. '*Tabaco, tabaco,*' they plead. I give them half a dozen cigarettes and some matches, and their faces light up immediately.

'*Dankie,*' one of them says. I am surprised to hear Afrikaans this far from South Africa. Another of them, a youth of about fourteen with a scraggly moustache on his upper lip and an RPG rocket-launcher strapped to his back offers me a drag from a rolled up smoke.

'*Tabaco?*' I ask. He waves his hand dismissively.

'*Bumu,*' he says. Whether it is a corruption of 'boom', the South African slang for marijuana, I don't know, but the sweet smell of the smoke confirms that it is the same stuff.

Seeing me refuse the offer of the dope, the third member of the trio, stoned out of his mind, starts cackling with laughter. He doubles over, holding his AK-47 at his waist. 'Uh-uh-uh-uh-uh-uh-uh'... he sweeps his gun past me in arc from the hip, his finger held loosely on the trigger, chattering in an imitation of machine-gun fire the way children who are playing war games do. His laughter becomes uncontrollable, and his companions drag him away giggling helplessly.

4

It is only seven o'clock in the morning. The sun is blazing overhead, and the sky is already bleached white from the glare. Without any visible signal, the convoy sets off. The trucks in front of us simply start moving off into the heat and we follow on. Already the sweat is running down Laxton's face, and outside the rolled-down windows of the cab the cicadas are starting to screech. Only a few kilometres down the road, we start to see evidence of the war that has wracked Mozambique for more than seventeen years. Every building along the side of the road is abandoned, roofless, the walls crumbling and shot through with holes from AK-47 fire and larger holes from rockets and canon shells. Then, around a corner in the bush, we see our first evidence of the more recent attacks: a huge load of bottles — a ton or more of them — lying in a glittering heap on the side of the road, the tarmac around black and burnt from rocket fire. '*Matsangas,*' Laxton says, pointing at the heap. Laxton travels this route at least once a month, but he doesn't know when that attack took place. What happened? How many people were hurt? How many people died here? Who were they?

The heat is building up and the road ahead is beginning to disappear in the shimmering layers of waves that form a continuous, shifting mirage.

5

About fifty kilometres out of Zobue is the most dangerous part of the journey. The bush is thick — mostly mopane — and the district is remote and utterly uninhabited — whether from the war or not I can't say, but there is no sign of huts or fields or bicycle tracks to point to the presence of humans, to break the screeching monotony of the cicadas, invisible in the thick bush.

It is in this area that most of the attacks take place, including the previous week's. The road is littered with the scorched wrecks of ambushed vehicles: the rusting, twisted skeleton of a container here; the charred remains of tyres and a smoke-blackened cab there; further along, a minibus with all its windows smashed and its doors riddled with bullet holes.

There is one particularly bad stretch where, for about twenty kilometres, every 500 metres or so, there is a burned-out vehicle lying in the bush on the side of the road. And all along the road are empty shell cases from heavy-machine guns. It is impossible not to feel the tension here, the soldiers ride up and down the convoy in their armoured vehicles peering anxiously into the bush, holding their weapons at the ready. The convoy we are in is made up of over a hundred trucks, each taking up at least fifty metres of road space, so that the line of trucks is five or six kilometres long, perhaps more. With only three vehicles guarding the convoy — one APC and two seven-ton trucks with machine guns mounted on the back — there are long periods of time when you are completely unprotected.

6

Cicadas. The roar of the engine. The heat. The constant, slow blur of the bush on the side of the road. If Renamo does hit you, it might take half an hour before the Frelimo escort even knows about it.

I remember something else Charlie told me. It was a piece of advice remembered from his days as a soldier in the Rhodesian war, something his sergeant had always told them:

'You don't have to worry about the bullet that has your name on it. The one you have to worry about is the one marked 'to whom it may concern'.

7

After two hours of driving we pull into Moatize, a small town on the outskirts of Tete. The town is desolate, mostly shanties and grass huts on the perimeter, and a few rundown houses from the Portuguese days in the centre of town. The APC comes screaming past us, headlights flashing, the horn blowing. In the back, the Frelimo soldiers give the 'thumbs up' sign at the drivers as they pass us. We are in Frelimo-secured territory again. Safe. A seven-ton truck with a machine gun on the back roars past us, headed for barracks in Tete. The same thing again: hooter blowing, the 'thumbs up' sign. It is only now, as they release the tension, that you realise how keyed-up the soldiers were.

8

Tete is a microcosm of a changing Mozambique. The houses are almost all relics of the colonial era, most of them crumbling and derelict, the peeling paint on the walls still the threadbare creams, pinks and blues of fifteen years ago, but the newest graffiti screams: *Rastaman* and *Stimela* — a South African band — the one faded graffito proclaiming *Viva Mocambique Independencia* is as old as the revolution itself.

The shelves of the main bookshop 'Liveria Popular' are almost empty. There are a few copies of Lenin's works, Gorbachev's 1986 address to the United Nations, and Portuguese translations of Rider Haggard's *She*. The doors of the town cathedral are barred. Inside, the nave is a mass of tumbled, smashed pews, and what remains of the altar is a bare wooden table covered in six-inch thick layers of pigeon shit. Yet there is a needlework class in the crypt, and a white Portuguese woman running a little convenience store across the courtyard. Outside, a shining new Toyota Hi-lux driven by a European aid worker on contract is parked next to a painted-over sign saying something in Portuguese about the decadence of the bourgeoisie. The streets are filled with potholes and littered with drink cans from South Africa: Fanta, Lemon Twist, Castle.

9

That night we sleep on the banks of the Zambezi near the suspension bridge within a few hundred metres of the old Portuguese slaving fort that dates back to 1648. Some of the drivers go to the newly-built *A Piscana* club on the edge of the Zambezi River. The club has a swimming pool and floodlit tennis courts, and you can eat barbecued chicken and drink Castle or the local Impala beer. All the latest music blares out from the speakers on the verandah: Madonna, Vanilla Ice and sultry, sexy Claire Johnston from Mango Groove '...*Moments away... You'll always be moments away from these arms...*'

Then, as the stars came out, and we are sitting in front of the club drinking beer, the throaty *craaak, craaak* of the giant bullfrogs almost drowns out the throb of the electronic music. Perhaps, smoothly gliding downstream, there is the red spark of a crocodile's eye caught in the gleam of the lights from the disco. And, in the darkness overlooking the club, there is the constant back-and-forth silhouette of Frelimo soldiers guarding the entrance to the bridge...

10

At 6:00 a.m. the next morning the heat is still there when the convoy starts to gather on the outskirts of town. To protect us, this morning there are 4 APCs, three seven-ton trucks with heavy-machine guns on the back, and two Land Rovers filled with troops.

The first section of the journey is not dangerous. The landscape is made up of a red sandy plain, dotted with thick knobbly baobabs. Here the extreme poverty of Mozambique is starkly evident. All along the road on this section are children standing begging, their hands outstretched towards the trucks as they drive past: 'Master, master,' they call to the drivers in pidgin English... 'Please bread, please bread... tobacco?... shirt?...' The children's' expressions contort in anger and disappointment as, one by one, the trucks crawl past them blowing dust and hot, reeking diesel fumes into their faces.

Further on, the bush becomes thicker and more remote. And the evidence of Renamo attacks is once again visible. A burned-out cab next to the blackened remains of a lala palm tree; a semi-trailer abandoned on the verge of the road. The mood starts to tighten up again. We have more protection than yesterday, but the possibility of an attack puts everyone on edge. The faces of the Frelimo troops are expressionless, but their eyes are red and lined beneath the rim of their helmets as they scan the bush on either side of the road.

11

In a shallow depression filled with white sand and sun-bleached grass there are the scorched remains of a Land Rover hit by an RPG-7 rocket. The rear section has a huge hole blasted out of the side, the steel skin pulverised into tiny paper-thin flakes of white ash. The passenger section of the cab is a blackened frame of metal ribs. The front tyre is flat, but the rubber is still good and pushed out firmly against the rim of the wheel.

'Yesterday,' Laxton says with authority, pointing at the Land Rover, and breaking the silence between us for the first time in half an hour.

'How do you know?' I ask.

He shrugs his shoulders, and smiles wryly. 'I heard last night.'

12

Twenty kilometres from the Zimbabwean border we come around a bend in the road. Just ahead of us is a column of thick black smoke rising into the air. All along the rise of the hill in front of us, the trucks are stopped and the drivers standing on the far edge of the road, peering anxiously ahead. There are no troops anywhere near us. A few drivers are gathered in anxious, jittery knots. The air is abuzz with a mix of Shona, English and Portuguese. Many of the drivers are on the verge of unhitching their loads and doing a U-turn. The bush around us is silent, and there is just the sight of the plume of smoke billowing up into the sky in front of us. There is no sound of gunfire, and so, the inexorable curiosity that the possibility of danger invites draws everyone on. No conscious decision is made, but the anxious groups of drivers break up and jog back to their trucks, they hoist themselves up into the cabs and, slamming the doors, and crashing the gears they start to crawl gingerly forward.

13

A few hundred metres on, there is a trailer burning furiously on the side of the road, a group of Frelimo soldiers is standing guard over it, AK-47s at the hip. A mounted machine gun is protecting the other side of the road, the crew is alert, the gunner has his finger on the trigger, and the barrels are lowered at the silent bush.

A few metres beyond that there is a horse standing without a trailer. Everybody gets out to gather around the driver and ask him what happened. He doesn't know, he didn't hear any shots, but he looked in his mirror and saw his cargo in flames. His hands are cut and bleeding from releasing his trailer so quickly, and he is still trembling with the shock.

His freight was bales of cotton, so the likely explanation for the fire is spontaneous combustion from the fibres rubbing together. But not everyone is convinced, and it is only when we reach the Zimbabwean border at Nyamapanda that the incident starts to fade and people start relaxing.

14

At the border at Nyamapanda, the incoming convoy meets up with the outgoing convoy. Three hundred or more trucks — 9000 tons of cargo caught up in a bureaucratic eddy of paperwork, smudged purple stamps, and large, officious signatures, and it is late in the afternoon before we are through the border at Nyamapanda.

A kilometre down the road from the border post into Zimbabwe is a pub where you can buy cold beer or cooldrinks. There is Lucky Dube blaring out of speakers on the wall, a snooker table in the corner, and young women sitting at the bar. Most of the drivers stop there for a drink, and the talk is all about the corridor. Who saw what, and where — a scorched wreck that hadn't been there last time they went through, a rustle someone saw in the mopane that had turned out to be hornbill — how scared nobody was... and, of course, what happened last week with the rockets, the bayonets and the pangas and what might have happened this week...

Many of the drivers are teetotallers, and deeply religious, but for others it's two, three, four pints and then back in the cab and rolling down the highway to Harare. Everybody handles it in his own way — it was only the fire this trip, but who knows what will happen next time? There are too many burnt-out wrecks along the road to think that it can't happen to you.

But, as Laxton will tell you, jobs are scarce in Zimbabwe, his wife and two daughters are waiting back home in Harare, and the danger pay for driving the Tete is 500 Zimbabwe dollars a trip.

CHAPTER 3

MOZAMBIQUE

PART 11 – SOMEWHERE SOUTH OF THE ZAMBEZI

He told me to call him Rodney, and I never did find out his real name. Although Rodney was incredibly secretive, I learned enough about him to see that he, in his own way, was an idealist, a man who believed that he was working for a better world, or, at least, a better southern Africa, and that his God had asked him to do this work. Rodney was also a good pilot who, by the very nature of his work, was brave enough to risk his life on a regular basis.

It must be said, though, that he did wear ridiculously tiny shorts.

Cameraman, Mike Purdy and I had been asked to do a story on Renamo. A cease-fire agreement was just about to be signed in Mozambique ending seventeen years of civil war, and for quite a while no one had been to their secret headquarters hidden deep in the forest somewhere in the Gorongosa National Park in central Mozambique. We were hired by an Italian television producer to do the story as there was increasing interest in Italy where the Mozambique peace talks were being held in Rome.

After a long series of phone calls back and forth between Rome, Blantyre, and Johannesburg, the pilot Rodney arrived at our hotel in Blantyre to pick us up. I had arranged with Rodney from Johannesburg that we would meet him at the hotel, and, from there, he would take us to the airport and then fly us to the secret Renamo base in central Mozambique.

Rodney put us in the back of his pick-up truck and drove us out to a little hangar on the edge of the runway. There were two black men pumping aviation fuel by hand into the wings of an old twin-engined aircraft standing on the tarmac. At the hotel, we'd greeted Rodney, and he'd replied, with the ubiquitous southern African 'Howzit!' and we'd not said a word to each other after that. Rodney was not much of a talker; part of it was that he was obviously determined to conceal his identity from us. Still, standing there rather uncomfortably on the tarmac watching him organise the loading of our luggage, sacks of rice, sugar and petrol into the plane, I thought we should at least try to make some small talk.

'What kind of plane is it?' I asked.

Rodney was checking something underneath the wing. He stood up and pushed his 1970s-John-Denver style glasses back up the bridge of his nose.

'Piper. Aztec.' He bent down again to continue whatever it was he had been doing before.

I tried again. 'And how old is it?'

Rodney looked up from underneath the shadow of the wing. He crooked his lips into a half-smile.

'About twenty-five years old.'

Rodney straightened up and clambered up onto the wing, his worn blue plastic flip-flops squishing out from underneath his heels as he found his balance again. He opened the door of the scratched and yellowed perspex cockpit and looked down at myself and Mike, still standing on the tarmac. He smiled again, more broadly this time: 'Wanna see the bullet hole in the floor?'

We took off and flew almost exactly due south. 'No photographs,' Rodney said as we lifted up into the air. I could read the figures on the GPS device clamped loosely to the dashboard. Mike was sitting up in the co-pilot's seat, chatting to Rodney. From the window of the cockpit I watched the shadow of the plane moving up and down over the fertile, well-tended slopes and valleys of southern Malawi. It wasn't long, perhaps fifteen, twenty minutes' flying time, before we crossed into Mozambique. I couldn't tell the exact moment we flew over the border, but it became obvious when we had left the cultivated order of Malawi behind and were flying over the wilderness of war-torn Mozambique. I knew there were people down there somewhere, but from the air there were, abruptly, no signs of human habitation — miles and miles of seemingly empty bush stretched out beneath us. Occasionally, I could see the shells of what had once been farmhouses, and were now nothing more than empty boxes of bare, bullet-riddled walls. Once, I saw a small bridge that had been destroyed, its concrete columns and cantilevered structures bent and twisted like crumpled paper.

'In the old days,' Rodney was telling Mike, 'sometimes somebody would try and shoot at us, but unless they actually hit you, you don't even know that it has happened.'

'And now?'

'No, not any more. Renamo controls all this territory beneath us. We're safe. They know we're coming.'

'How do they know?'

'They know.' Rodney lapsed into silence again. The last question had come too close to the boundaries of what he wanted to protect. We flew for a while without saying anything until Rodney himself offered the next comment.

'Renamo controls about 85% of the countryside. They've got Frelimo holed up in the major cities.' Was it true? No one really knew. Certainly, most of the news coming out of Mozambique came exclusively from a few correspondents based in Frelimo-controlled Maputo, over 800 kilometres to the south of where we were. Reliable information about Renamo was extremely difficult to get.

Rodney continued, pointedly: 'The press hates us, but Renamo is supported by 80% of the Mozambican people. One day, somebody will tell the real story. Until then, I'll keep flying for the Movement. It's my contribution. I do it because God wants me to do it.'

'How many other pilots do the same thing?'

'Ah, well, there's quite a few of us now. The Movement is growing all the time.'

On the one hand, they were pat, easy answers. He said nothing about the scores of documented atrocities committed by Renamo fighters. There was no doubt about the truth of these accounts — the sources were varied and reliable. They came from refugees, Western aid workers, journalists, diplomats. Renamo was guilty of serious human rights abuses on a large scale in Mozambique. In addition, Rodney's refusal to even mention them smacked of the sort of willful avoidance of an unpleasant reality that did more to tacitly confirm the view that Renamo was responsible for the attacks than to deny it. On the other hand, from a journalistic point of view, it had to be acknowledged that what was less certain, was exactly who was responsible for each individual atrocity. There were also some reports that renegade Frelimo troops had committed atrocities, and that the information had largely been hushed up.

Rodney's answers also had a ring of personal sincerity about them. Whatever anyone else might have thought about Renamo and what he was doing, *he* was convinced that he was doing the right thing.

Sure, he was getting paid for what he did, but he was also genuinely putting his life in danger by regularly flying this rickety old plane over miles of remote, war-torn bush. On the face of it, one had to respect the fact that he was a man who was acting on his beliefs.

We flew for half an hour; an hour. The terrain below flattened out and became dry, grey savannah with dead grass and miles of withered thorn trees that cast thin, lacy shadows on the parched red earth.

'Look there,' Rodney said, pointing. The Zambezi lay in the sand ahead of us like a glistening silver ribbon. Rodney dipped the wing and flew low over a sandbank to give us a view of some hippos lying in the shallows — beautiful, glistening animals next to a grove of palm trees. A scene older than humanity itself, and then we were across the river. The dusty plain and the thorn trees stretched out in front of us; the blue sky arched over the cockpit like a bubble of water. Both Mike and I fell asleep.

The motion of the plane changed, kinking over to starboard and pushing me sideways in my seat. I woke up and hurriedly looked at the liquid crystal display on the GPS device, but I didn't know how long I had been asleep or how many times we might have changed direction since we crossed the Zambezi. So much for my plan to keep track of our movements. I had no idea where we were. We were flying over forest now, and, suddenly, in amongst the trees, appeared a narrow landing strip hacked out of the forest. Rodney throttled back and began the descent. A few moments later, we were bumping across the grassy runway, the engines screaming, the smell of aviation fuel filling the cockpit.

As we hit the ground, I noticed a few ragged soldiers standing at intervals in the bush along the edge of the runway with their AK-47s clutched to their chests. They didn't look very savoury, and they weren't wearing uniforms at all, just ripped, dirty T-shirts and jeans, shorts or rotting combat fatigues. Most of them were barefoot or wearing unbelievably tattered combat boots or running shoes. They looked just like the bandits the government accused them of being.

I felt a small spasm of anxiety rush through my chest. I suddenly wasn't sure what we were getting ourselves into. Renamo had kidnapped other journalists and aid workers before — in one of the most well-known cases, cameraman Nick Della Casa had been with them for eight months before he was finally set free. Still, it was too late to back out now. The nervousness passed and turned into excitement — the heady, addictive flow of curiosity in its purest, distilled form.

Rodney kept the propellers turning. 'Can't afford to let them pack up here,' he said over the roar of the engines. We climbed down from the plane and some of the soldiers came forward to help us with our baggage. Rodney unloaded the supplies he had brought and then scrambled back up the wing. A group of soldiers gathered around the plane and Rodney spoke to them fluently in what sounded like Shona (many of the soldiers were Ndaus, whose language is a dialect of Shona) without a hint of the pidgin, stumbling condescension that characterises the speech of so many whites who claim to speak an African language.

Before he left, though, I thought I'd better check our travel plans one more time. 'We'll see you in three days?' I shouted up at him.

'Don't worry,' he yelled back; and then: 'It's a long walk back to Jo'burg, hey?'

We watched the plane taxi down the frighteningly short runway and climb into the sky. Rodney was gone, and his absence was a constant reminder that we were utterly reliant on him to pick us up again. We didn't even know his real name, and yet we had to trust him implicitly. If anything happened to either one of us — any small accident, a broken ankle perhaps, or a stick from one of the trees in the forest gashing an exposed eyeball — before we could get anything but the most rudimentary treatment, we would have to wait for Rodney and his flimsy plane to return.

The soldiers led us into the shade of the forest. The bush was uncannily green and thick, and the trees, panga-panga, mahogany, ironwood, towered over us, creating an over-arching canopy of cool shade. It was almost a prehistoric landscape, with deep, shadowed greens and soft, fertile soil. Six-inch long land snails with brightly striped shells glided silently across the cool forest floor; huge shiny black songololos crawled up the trunks of the trees, their thousand legs a shuffling carpet of crimson, their brown antennae wiggling constantly in front of them. This whole area had once been a game park, thronged with elephant, buffalo and rhino, but they had almost all been shot in the war. Ivory and rhino horn bought guns; buffalo and antelope gave meat for the soldiers; only the plants and the insects remained.

There were three Honda scramblers with soldiers at the handlebars waiting in the forest shade. An officer in green fatigues carrying a rusty Makarov pistol in a holster made of leopard fur motioned for us to get up on the bikes behind the soldiers, while he got on the third bike. The other soldiers put our suitcases and the supplies Rodney had brought on their heads and set off on foot through the trees. The three of us roared off in single file along a narrow forest path; dust and thick, two-stroke engine smoke from the bike ahead of me

flew up into my eyes; overhanging branches whipped past my
face in a blur as we slipped and careened dangerously close to
the trunks of rare African hardwoods. The likelihood of that
small but serious accident occurring was even greater than I
had thought. I tried to watch the odometer on the handlebars
in front of me. The kilometres clicked by in trendy day-glo
yellow: one, two, three, four...

After thirty minutes or so, we emerged from the gloom of
the deep forest and roared into a clearing. There were a few
men in both uniforms and neat civilian clothes standing
around in front of a large open pavilion. It had waist-level
mud walls and a sloping thatched roof. Dotted around the
edges of the clearing were a few other huts with reed walls and
grass roofs. Our drivers took us on a bucking, skidding
ceremonial circuit of the clearing and then came to a wobbly
halt in front of the pavilion. Almeida Dos Santos, 'Vice Head
of Information Department' stepped forward to meet us. He
was wearing a white civilian shirt and dark-blue slacks. His
eyes were hidden by imitation Ray-Ban Wayfarers. He
extended his right hand in greeting; in the other, he held a
shortwave radio with the aerial extended. 'I'm here to answer
all your questions,' he told us. 'Renamo has no secrets.'

We went into the pavilion and sat down at a large wooden
table for a briefing from Almeida. Women soldiers dressed in
combat boots, neatly-pressed army shirts and colourful
African wrap skirts brought us coffee and condensed milk.
While we sipped the hot, sweet coffee, we discussed our
schedule for the next few days. Mike, of course, was eager to
get as many pictures as he could, so he led the discussion as to
what exactly there was that we could film.

'The camp, the hospital, the military school...'

'What about filming soldiers?'

'No problem. You can even film our women soldiers
training if you want to. Renamo has many women soldiers;
they are often our best fighters.'

One thing we were particularly keen to film was their
communications centre, for two reasons: firstly, there were
many rumours that radio equipment had recently been
supplied to Renamo from South Africa; secondly, and, from

Renamo's point of view, more positively, it was clear that despite their execrable human rights record, Renamo simply were not the lawless bandits that they were made out to be. There were a number of indications that Renamo was adhering to certain (by no means all) of the many regional cease-fire agreements that had been signed in the last couple of years. Renamo was also waging a fairly successful guerrilla campaign. The probable secret behind both of these factors was an efficient communications centre, and to film it would be a minor 'scoop' for the two of us.

'No problem,' Almeida told Mike. 'You can film it tomorrow. Renamo has no secrets.'

That night we had dinner of venison stew, rice and beans in the pavilion with Almeida and few other Renamo officials. While we were eating, the women standing around the table suddenly snapped to attention. The men sitting at the table got up out of their chairs and stood to attention as well. Afonso Dhlakama, the Renamo leader, emerged out of the darkness surrounding the pavilion. He was dressed in camouflage fatigues with smart red lapels, a black beret and shiny combat boots. Mike and I stood up to greet him. My immediate impression was of a quiet, mild-mannered man who shook our hands warmly − not at all the bloodthirsty ogre he had been so often painted as. But of course, social niceties mean nothing − who knows what lies beneath the smooth unruffled facade that any politician creates? Finding that out is finding the real story. We knew that our ability to find it with Dhlakama and Renamo would be extremely limited − for a start, we were stuck in the remotest bush literally hundreds of miles away from the nearest town, and we were totally in the hands of Renamo. We knew we would see only what they wanted us to see, and hear only what they wanted us to hear but, nonetheless, we were determined to try and see and hear for ourselves, to uncover as much of the truth as we could.

It was with this in mind that we shook Dhlakama's hand and chatted to him for a few brief moments before he took his leave of us and disappeared back into the night. Both Mike and I tried to remain properly distant, but, at the same time, respectful. We were certainly not there to be sucked into Renamo's public relations machine, as crude as it appeared to be, but we were also not there simply to gather material to condemn them. We had come, hopefully with an open mind, to get the real story — or, at least, to get as close to it as we could.

After dinner Mike and I were shown to one of the huts on perimeter of the clearing which was to be our home for the next few days. Two beds made of logs and covered with simple foam mattresses and clean sheets and army blankets stood at the one end of the hut; at the other was a sort of dressing table made also of logs and on it stood a jug of water and a galvanized tin basin. A single naked bulb hung from the roof that ran on electricity provided by a generator hidden a little way off among the trees. Every time we moved, it cast huge, looming shadows against the reed walls of our hut. The hut had been put up directly on top of the sandy forest floor, so when you climbed into bed you had to perform a number of carefully thought out contortions in order to take off your pants and keep the sand off your feet, and remove your socks also without getting sand on your feet. Then you had to change into your sleeping shorts (definitely without getting sand in them) and finally lift your sandless feet onto the bed. God help you if you wanted to get up in the middle of the night for a pee.

The lights went out abruptly at 10:00. At first the whole interior of the hut was plunged into the darkness of the forest night; by the time our eyes had gotten used to the gloom the walls and roof of our hut were crawling with vermin. We could hear them constantly scuttling through the reeds just next to our beds and dropping tiny fragments of grass and bark on our heads and faces as they slithered through the straw of the roof. At first, I shone the beam of my torch in the direction of the noises. The rats, and worse, were too quick for me, but I saw geckos with shiny black eyes and long suckery toes arranged into large flat, scurrying feet; hovering in the darkness above us, mosquitoes the size of tarantulas (I have the word *literally* underlined several times in my notebook); and, silently clinging to the rough-hewn rafters, huge black and orange spiders with hairy, thick legs long enough to encompass half a large apple.

After the spiders, I stopped using my torch. The only thing to do was to get drunk and bury one's head under the blankets. Luckily, we had thought to bring along a half-bottle of brandy.

'Women soldiers,' Almeida told us at breakfast. 'You can film women soldiers today.'

'And the radio room?' Mike asked.

'Tomorrow, definitely.'

First, we were taken on a tour of the camp. It was well-laid out and must have been invisible from the air. The huts of the 400 or so workers and soldiers based there were spaced out for protection against air attack along the narrow footpaths that wound through the tall trees. Dhlakama's complex at the centre of the camp consisted of an office, his personal quarters, the row of huts we were sleeping in and a kitchen compound. The whole arrangement had the atmosphere of a somewhat rustic safari camp. Deeper into the forest, there was a small parade ground, a large straw church, a small clinic, a tailor shop and, Almeida's pride and joy, an information centre operating with the aid of an old hand-cranked copying machine and two ancient manual typewriters.

Most of the Renamo soldiers were ragged and dressed in whatever clothes they could find, but the women soldiers were always better dressed than the men. They all carried battered and rusted AK-47 rifles and often a patched and torn half-bag of mealie-meal or personal possessions on their heads, but whenever we, or an officer, passed them in the forest, the soldiers would step off the path and snap smartly to attention.

I asked Almeida where they got their weapons from. He smiled. 'We capture them from the enemy, of course.' And the motorbikes?

'We must hurry. The women soldiers will be drilling soon. We don't want you to miss that.'

'*Viva Dhlakama, nosso presidente…*' The women soldiers were in two neat rows, marching up and down an open plain that was surrounded by trees some distance from the camp. They were singing loudly and their boots thumped down on the ground in time with the rhythm of the song. It was an impressive sight and Mike was getting great pictures. They repeated their manoeuvres two or three times in order for Mike to get the cutaways he needed, and then they came to a halt at the edge of the clearing.

'Now they will strip their weapons and . . .' Almeida began; but, rising above the drone of insects in the mid-morning heat, we could just hear the sound of a plane.

'It's the pilot,' Almeida said. 'He's coming back.' We looked up, above the line of the forest. We could see the plane as a tiny dot in the hazy, white sky. It moved slowly across the horizon and then disappeared behind a tree-covered rise some kilometres away. 'There are some more guests coming,' Almeida told us, and then we went back to the women soldiers, the stripping of the rifles and then, in Portuguese, the naming of parts.

When we arrived back at the camp for lunch, there were five white men, and Rodney, seated at the table in the shade of the pavilion. All of them, with the exception of a professional photographer called Al Vargas who had been commissioned to do some work on Renamo, were supporters of The Movement. There was an overweight, bespectacled Englishman called David; a university professor called something like Gunther, a little-spoken South African called Alan from 'Bophuthatswana' (he talked of it in absolute earnestness as if it were truly an independent country), and a Zimbabwean called Brian.

We got off the motorbikes, hot, dusty; Mike, who had been on the scrambler behind mine, had his face covered in black soot from the exhaust. We were introduced to them, and we all shook hands politely. Rodney nodded at us from across the table and said nothing. We sat down at the table and the group fell into an uncomfortable silence. David Hoile, I found out later, was a figure of some notoriety in Britain. A brilliant young man, but a Conservative with such radical views that Margaret Thatcher herself had drummed him out of the party, he had turned his attentions to southern Africa instead, and had recently created the 'Mozambique Institute' based in London which was dedicated to promoting Renamo's cause abroad. Our new additions were a mixed bag, certainly, and none of them, with the exception of Al, wanted much to do with Mike and me. They stuck to themselves mostly, only speaking to us when it would have been ridiculously impolite not to do so.

Dhlakama joined us at dinner in the pavilion that evening, sitting at the head of the table in an ornate carved wooden chair. A relic of colonial days, the wood was filled with hundreds of pinhead-sized holes where borer beetles had chewed a network of tiny tunnels to lay their eggs. Two uniformed bodyguards stood stiffly behind him, staring straight ahead, their new AK-47s held diagonally across their chests.

There was bread on the table, and flower-print enamel bowls of antelope stew. Three or four women soldiers stood nearby to serve us. Almeida and few other Renamo officials were joining us for dinner so we spaced ourselves around the table and sat down.

'Let us pray,' Brian said. 'Lord Jesus, we ask you to bless this bread...' When the prayer was over, we passed the stew and the bread around in an atmosphere of uncomfortable silence. No one seemed to know what to say. I sensed a certain impatience among the Renamo officials, most of whom had almost certainly been brought up with a blend of African traditional beliefs and Portuguese Catholicism, with the Mid-West American-style Protestantism of Brian and Alan and Rodney, and perhaps this contributed to some of the uneasiness.

The other factor was Dhlakama's obvious shyness. For a start, his English was not all that good, and most of us spoke nothing more than a few words of Portuguese. He seemed bored and frustrated with having to share this wordless dinner with his guests, but, at the same time, one could sense that he knew it was his duty, for the Movement's sake.

The few times that Dhlakama did speak, the whole table fell silent. With the exception of myself, Mike and Al (who kept his own counsel), the attitude of everyone at the table towards Dhlakama was respectful in the extreme, and they listened in silence to every word he said. The people gathered around this table, black and white, shared a common political vision that, in the end, had nothing to do with race. That was certainly the way it appeared at dinner that night, and, after having known all of them for only a few hours, I was in no position to judge them or to say that it was not true.

At one point in the dinner, Dhlakama turned and spoke specifically to Mike and me.

'It is important for you to understand the aims and principles of Renamo. We are not trying to put Frelimo out of power; we are fighting for a multi-party democracy. Of course, if the people vote us into power then we will govern.'

But why keep fighting? Why keep the war going on?

'We want peace, but we cannot just stop fighting. We must have our principles recognised first, otherwise what have we spent fourteen years in the bush for? What have we had thousands of our people killed for?'

'The war,' said Almeida, 'is the only reason Frelimo is negotiating with us at all.'

The conversation was clearly over. It was only when the talk moved on, that I happened to glance over at Rodney. His face was a mask of inscrutability, but he also looked very ill.

Dhlakama took his leave and the dinner ended. Rodney excused himself too, and the rest of us, including the other Renamo officials, somehow ended up watching videos in the pavilion. The picture quality was awful, but the variety of programmes was quite astonishing. There seemed very little logic attached to the timing and order of the recordings. We would be watching a Jackie Chan Kung Fu movie and then suddenly P.J. Powers, a white South African singer, would storm across the screen, or Tiffany, or a commercial for MacDonalds ('A very famous restaurant in America,' Almeida told me).

While we watched, huge African bugs crawled across the screen. Attracted by the flickering light of the tube, they would land on Gloria Estefan's face, their long, jointed antennae caressing her gorgeous lips until someone could stand it no longer, and would get up off his chair and flick the creature off the screen. But always, homing in from the darkness, there were more insects — a constant, chaotic stream of crawling life that was like the erratic drip of a tap that, in the end, will wear away the hardest stone.

David was as bored by the TV as I was, and the two of us ended up talking alone at the other end of the pavilion, away from the television set.

'Of course there are atrocities,' he admitted. 'But the thing is, they happen on both sides. After all, there's a war going on, isn't there?'

And how big did he think Renamo was, really?

'It's very big, but no one knows how big, really.'

Now where did they get their supplies from?

He smiled, and didn't answer.

I was genuinely curious about Rodney. 'The pilot, he seems quite committed. There can't be many like him.'

'There aren't. He's the only one. He's the only way they can get out of here. Without him, there would be no negotiations in Rome, no peace talks at all.'

And, presumably then, although he didn't say it, also no fuel or spares for the motorbikes and the generator, no paper for the copying machines, no batteries for the shortwave radios, no medical supplies, no pop videos, no sugar for the endless cups of coffee… it all seemed too much for one man. And what about the supplies that really mattered? The AK-47s and ammunition, the RPGs, the hand grenades, the mortars? Certainly, Rodney's small plane could have carried very few weapons indeed, and the tiny landing strip we used could not have accommodated a plane any larger. No, there was much, much more to this story than that. I looked at David smiling at me in the yellow glow of the one electric bulb hanging above us. I wondered how much he really knew about this story; and, how much there was that he didn't know.

The electricity shut off, and with it Gloria Estefan's smile. Brian, Alan and the others disappeared into the darkness. Mike and I were going to our hut for a quiet brandy and we asked Al if he wanted some as well. Almeida and one or two of the other Renamo officials were hanging around, rather pointedly, it seemed. They had obviously found out about our brandy, and, even if they hadn't, it would have been churlish not to ask them to join us.

Almeida and the others went to bring chairs, a table and an assortment of chipped glasses. While they were away, Al leaned over in the darkness towards me: 'I think you'd better be careful about what you ask. They don't like it. I would be very careful about it if I were you. Remember, you're in their hands.'

We sat down outside our hut with only a flickering hurricane lamp for light (at least it didn't attract too many insects) and Mike poured out a small tot of brandy for everyone.

'This is good brandy,' Almeida said, holding up the glass to the lamplight. 'Is it South African? The pilot usually won't bring any alcohol on the plane.'

'Well,' I said, 'he didn't know about this one.'

Everyone laughed, and Almeida made a face in the half-light of the hurricane lamp. We sat around the table talking about inconsequential things. Clearly, none of the Renamo officials was much of a drinker, and they all got tipsy quite quickly. The evening began to break up when Almeida and one of the other Renamo men got embroiled in a long discussion comparing Portuguese, English and French grammar. The debate ended when the brandy ran out, and we all started to go our separate ways towards our huts. We were leaving the next day, and Mike decided to try once more:

'About the radio room, do you think it would be possible... just a few shots?'

'No problem,' Almeida said, lifting his left arm up in a cheery wave. 'No problem at all. Tomorrow, definitely, tomorrow...' He disappeared into the darkness with his shortwave radio held unsteadily in his right hand.

'Forget about it,' Al said. 'They probably don't have one, and if they do, they're never going to let you film it.'

The next morning Rodney was not at breakfast. 'He's down with a bout of malaria,' Brian announced. 'I've been doing what I can, but there's not much I can do. Just make sure he's got plenty of liquids and keep the fever down.'

'Is he going to be all right?' Almeida asked. His eyes were invisible behind his sunglasses, but it was obvious that he had a hangover. Mike and I looked at each other. We had a deadline in Italy for the story. Television has a gluttonous appetite, but the attention span of a gnat — a delay of even a day or two here would seriously jeopardise the chances of the story even appearing on air.

'He's been through this many times before. I'm sure he'll be all right. They don't come as tough as he does.'

After breakfast we all (except Al who had gone off to photograph the camp) waited in the shade for our turn with Dhlakama. We wanted an on-camera interview but before us, each one of the others was getting a private audience with him. Dhlakama, dressed in neatly-pressed combat fatigues and black beret, was sitting at the table in the pavilion, a large sheaf of papers in front of him, and the two bodyguards standing behind him.

We waited; none of us spoke. Almeida sat under a tree a little way off, listening to his short-wave radio. First, the professor was called over to the pavilion, then Alan — a short meeting — then Brian, and David — a much longer session.

Of course, Mike and I were dying to know what was actually being said at these meetings. The others all sensed our eagerness, but they also knew that we would never know the content of their discussions, and so the joke was on us.

The meetings took a couple of hours to complete, and, at the end, Rodney even came out of his hut to have his meeting with Dhlakama. His was the longest of all. We watched from a distance as the late morning grew hotter and hotter and the forest shadows started shortening across the sandy floor. Blue-tailed skinks with black eyes scuttled up and down the tree trunks and a redchested cuckoo whistled its lonely, rhythmic call somewhere off in the forest: *piet-my-vrou, piet-my-vrou, piet-my-vrou*. Dhlakama wrote something on a piece of paper and passed it across the table to Rodney, who looked at it for a long time before saying anything. The two of them together bent over a map, another piece of paper, sat back in their chairs again, and laughed. They stood up and shook hands; the meeting was over. Rodney came over to where Mike and I were sitting; he was clearly feeling better, his eyes were gleaming behind his spectacles.

'The President will see you now,' he told us. 'But you'd better make it quick, I'm leaving in an hour.'

The interview, predictably, was disappointing, filled with carefully thought-out sound bites:

'We want a multi-party democratic system where people can see two, three, four parties and they can choose which party they want through voting...'

'The whole population of Mozambique supports Renamo, including all members of Frelimo except a few ministers who are orthodox, also, you must consider that in the Renamo-controlled territory we have seven and a half million people who automatically support us...'

And what about the many confirmed reports of massive human rights violations by Renamo?

'People accuse us of being bandits, of killing civilians, cutting off ears, mutilating babies — of terrible things. But we are not worried about that because our people — the fifteen million Mozambicans know that Renamo are not bandits. One day, the outside world will know that they have received the wrong information about us. We need an election here, an election in Mozambique will show the world who really killed the civilians.'

The plane took off and climbed over the forest canopy. As it banked and turned towards the blue sky above us, I thought about something that had happened just before we got on the plane. Mike had been making small talk with Rodney while we waited for the luggage to be stowed.

'Dhlakama seems to be quite friendly,' Mike said, an inconsequential, conversational remark.

'Ja,' Rodney had replied. 'He's not a bad guy — for a munt.'

Not a bad guy − for a munt. In the light of everything that had gone before, the mind boggles, scrabbles for meaning around this remark. It was something akin to, say, one of Jesse Jackson's white campaign trail aides calling him a 'nigger' in private. We had all the details and quotes that would appear in our television and newspaper reports, but here was the real story. How was it possible that a man, like Rodney, who seemed, at least on the surface, to have so much respect for the man Afonso Dhlakama − who certainly regularly risked his life for him and for his movement, Renamo, could still call him, so casually, so easily: *a munt?* Did Dhlakama and Almeida know, I wondered, that Rodney (and the others, too?) spoke about them like that? And if they did, then who, in the end, was using whom?

Or, was it after all, nothing but a joke − a bad, silly joke?

We flew low over a village on the bone-dry savannah below. The people came out to wave at us. They stood there in the dusty centre of their circle of huts, looking up into the air at the plane. The children were jumping up and down in excitement and the adults, some of whom were dressed in nothing more than a tattered grain sack, were waving their arms wildly above their heads as we approached them. Rodney smiled and waved back from the cockpit. As we flew directly overhead, he dipped the wing of his plane down as an answer to their waving, and then they were behind us, gone from our lives for ever.

The plane straightened out, and I watched Rodney sitting in the pilot's seat. He was absorbed in the business of flying, staring at his instrument panel, squinting his eyes in concentration behind his glasses, every now and then reaching down and making some minor adjustment.

I looked at the compass. We were on course. In an hour or so, we would be crossing the Zambezi. We would make the deadline. In a few days, Afonso Dhlakama would be addressing the world through its television screens.

CHAPTER 4

MOZAMBIQUE

PART 111 – A SEASON OF HUNGER

15

The grass was as tall as a man on the peaks of the Lebombo mountains on the border between South Africa and Mozambique. When the wind came up, the long grass stems swayed and rustled in the currents of air, and you could hear the chatter of small birds and insects looking for food among the stalks.

In the valleys far below, the sugar cane and banana fields of the South African farmers made up a rich green patchwork that stretched west as far as the eye could see. It is a rich country and a man or a woman might easily find work there. And so they came, in their thousands, in their tens of thousands, to cross the Lebombo mountains where, on the other side, there was work and food for one's children and peace from the fighting...

But since 1986 there had been a new sound on the mountaintops: the eerie, high-pitched wail of the wind whistling through the sharp blades of razor wire. Along the border from Komatipoort to Swaziland there is a fence that was built to keep the people from Mozambique out.

For now, the fence is switched off. But at that time on some days 2000 volts ran through the coils of razor wire, on other days lower, non-lethal voltage ran through it, and on some days it was switched off altogether. You never knew what the situation was on a given day. It was the final hurdle in the long walk from the war-torn villages of Mozambique, but it did not stop the people coming. They didn't try to get over the fence or go through it. Specially hired guides showed them how to prop up the fence with sticks and crawl underneath.

16

There were those who tried to cross it without guides.

'Often they had been there for days. We had to sort of push and pull at the bodies with long wooden sticks to get them off the razor wire,' a friend of mine who had done part of his national service on the Mozambique border recalled once, late at night, when he was drunk. 'And then we had to load them onto trucks and they took them away to bury them.'

17

Patrick's mother was killed in a Renamo attack on his village when he was thirteen. He found his mother's dead body. What happened to his father is not clear, but Patrick says that his father is living in Maputo now. Patrick and his friend walked to the border where they were confronted by the fence. Patrick does not remember clearly what happened after he touched it. He knows his hand was burnt so badly that the flesh melted off the bone in places. The power of the shock pushed him into the coils of razor wire and his arms and legs and back and stomach were deeply lacerated. 'My friend tried to push me off with a stick,' he says. 'And then I was unconscious. The next day two soldiers found me. They took me to hospital where the doctor had to cut my hand off.'

18

It was as Father Gaetan, a French Canadian missionary who worked with the refugees, had said: 'These people have nothing. For them, South Africa is a little corner of Paradise.'

19

The plane banked over Maputo harbour in preparation for
the final approach to the airport. The water in the bay seemed
alternatively deep and shallow, in the deep patches it was
blue, but in other parts it was dirty with brownness of mud
and the sudden whiteness of a sandbank that had almost
reached the surface. Rotting skeletons of ships lay abandoned
in the middle of the harbour, the tiny white tips of waves
breaking against their rusting sides.

At the edge of the bay, the city glistened in the sparkling
sun, the white skyscrapers gleaming against the blue African
sky, and the turquoise sea seeming to lap almost against the
edge of the golden beaches. From the air, Maputo was a
gleaming metropolis shimmering on the edge of waking from
some barely-remembered dream.

20

The entire length of the road from the airport into town was
lined on either side with a shanty town. Myself as soundman,
Dave Spiro as cameraman and correspondent Tom Carver
had come to Mozambique to report for BBC World Service
Television. Our taxi sped past endless rows of flimsy straw and
dried palm-leaf structures and rusting corrugated-iron
shacks. People, chickens and goats wandered in and out of
its tiny, garbage-strewn alleyways — the archetypal scene of
African poverty.

21

Still, since Frelimo had officially abandoned Marxism in 1990
things were getting better. At the open-air markets in
Maputo, there were plenty of things for sale, almost anything
you wanted: clothes, paraffin, videos, beer, whiskey, grain,
flour, salt, fruit, cashews...

There was building going on all over the city, people
refurbishing the old colonial mansions, building apartment
blocks, fixing small sections of an apartment section by

section. There were shining new cars all over town, and smart young couples dining in the open-air restaurants that had been reopened all down the Avenue Julius Nyrere. Dozens of them were, of course, the ex-pat aid workers whose injections of aid-money and personal salaries had so artificially inflated the local Maputo economy, but just as many of the couples were Mozambicans — the new bourgeoisie. Things were definitely getting better in Maputo, there was no question of that.

22

The British Embassy in Maputo is a tasteful, colonial-style structure with a red-tiled roof and white shutters to keep out the heat, set in a garden of palms and bright tropical flowers. Tom Carver and I arrived one night after an invitation from the ambassador for a briefing on the situation in Mozambique.

We were led into the elegant drawing room that seemed to have remained intact from an earlier part of this century. The walls were a subdued lemon and eggshell blue with the trim and the ornamental moulding on the ceiling painted white. The spaces of the room were filled with treasures drawn from all the corners of the old empire: blue and white porcelain vases from China, an imposing mahogany glass-fronted armoire was filled with silver artefacts and deep ruby and navy blue Oriental rugs lay on top of the carpeted floor.

We sat down with the ambassador and the British military attaché for Mozambique.

'This is the same house, you know,' said the ambassador as he fixed our drinks — gin and tonics — 'that Winston Churchill took refuge in when he escaped from imprisonment in the Transvaal during the Boer War, and fled here to Maputo, then called Lourenço Marques, of course.'

The military attaché was sitting opposite me, a thin anxious man in his late fifties or early sixties. Mozambique was probably his last career posting. He seemed something of a sad man, dressed shabbily in the faded veneer of British authority, an old lacklustre regimental tie, a worn, slightly frayed collar, and mismatching socks — one a sort of Leander pink, the other a slightly dirty Cambridge blue.

'It's difficult to say who controls what here, or how much,' he told us, halfway through our gin and tonics. 'Renamo seems to be trying to make some sort of last push to gain territory before the ceasefire. They'll probably take some towns, but they'll never be able to hold them. But, at the same time, the government doesn't have the strength to push them back. Probably only 10% of the land is held by anybody, the rest of the country is a fluid no-man's land, possession of which changes hands constantly.'

And the atrocities? 'Absolutely certain. There are massive human rights abuses all across the country. Just this week I was on a visit upcountry. I met a young boy who was kidnapped by Renamo at a railway siding when he was still very young. A few years later, they took him back to the town he had come from at night and told him to fire at a certain house on a certain street corner. When he came back to his commander to report that he had carried out his mission, they told him that it was his parents' house. They told him he had just killed his parents and there was no going back now.'

But there are reports of atrocities coming from the Frelimo side.

'Must be, but Renamo bears the bulk of the responsibility. There's absolutely no doubt in my mind about that. What you've got here is the worst insurgency in the world fighting the worst army in the world. It's tragic. The situation is desperate. Food has become the most powerful weapon in Mozambique.

'But,' I protested, 'things seem to be getting better here than they were the last time I was in Mozambique.'

'Maputo,' he said, 'Maputo is fine. You have to go to the provinces to see the suffering.'

23

The blue Indian Ocean lapped against the white beach. On the water, men and boys in dugout canoes skillfully negotiated the breakers to bring the morning's catch in.

Behind us, the Hotel Dom Pedro, once the jewel in Beira's holiday crown, was a dilapidated ruin with shattered windows and filth coating the walls. The lighthouse on the beach next to us, built in 1927, no longer served any useful purpose; its light had stopped warning ships years ago.

'The war,' said Moussa, our guide and driver in Beira, 'is our biggest problem. The government followed communism, and look what has happened.' He turned and pointed at the hotel and the lighthouse. He chose his next words carefully. 'Renamo,' he said, 'is fighting communism. After the war is over, we will be free to choose between them.'

24

The ground in Chibabava, 150 kilometres inland from Beira, was dry, dry, dry. There was nothing but fine powdery dust and dead leaves on the ground. There had been no rain here for months, and the people were starving, crawling out of the bush like ghosts to get grain from the tiny ICRC outpost here.

The extent of the famine outside Maputo was horrifying, the people here were literally shuffling, barely walking, hardly living skeletons. Their arms and legs dried, hollow sticks; their faces drawn tight against the bones of their skulls. The women's breasts hung down in flaps of skin as thin as the leather tongue of a large boot; the men were clutching onto sticks and struggling to carry their tiny bundles of personal possessions; the children were thin and coughing, clinging to their mothers, their eyes encrusted with jewel-like rings of flies devouring the moisture underneath their eyelids. Underneath the disgusting circles of these rapacious insects, the childrens' eyes were not dull and listless, like one reads so often; instead, they were sharp, and bright with fear.

25

Two old women were kneeling on the ground outside a hut. The sun was beating down mercilessly on them. Their skin had been so damaged by a combination of disease and malnutrition it was peeling off their shoulders and backs in huge curling brown sheets. The ICRC workers had treated the raw patches with gentian violet, but there was not much else they could do. The women were crawling slowly around in circles in the dust, unable to sit or lie because of the extreme pain.

The ICRC workers told us that the government had put mines around the town, both to protect it from Renamo and to prevent Renamo sympathisers inside the town from slipping out to join forces with those outside. It was these minefields that the starving refugees had to walk through to come to get help from the ICRC. Last night alone, two people had their legs blown off by the mines.

In addition, the minefields stopped the people returning to the bush with food for their relatives outside the town, so the problem grew worse by the day. Without the food, the starvation outside increased and so more people were forced to come into the town, but then they could not leave again, and there was not enough food and medicine to treat the thousands who were there already.

26

An eerie silence filled the air over the camp. There was nothing but the sound of the wind rustling in the dry leaves of the trees; the listless thud of a single wooden pestle and mortar crushing grain; the thin, subdued wail of a baby with hardly enough energy to cry. It disappeared and the thud of the pestle stopped too. An old lady with her skin so wrinkled it resembled the ravages of burn-scars pulled a calabash towards her and lifted it with both hands up to her mouth to drink. As she drank, water poured down her chin, onto her lap and dribbled away into the grey, dry soil.

27

At the aid distribution point, fights broke out as the absolute need for food overwhelmed people in a sudden, uncontrol-lable wave. They were ghastly and pathetic at the same time, these fights — the churning, jerky movements of people too weak with hunger to hurt one another, but within whom the desire to continue living at almost any cost burned fiercely. The Mozambicans working for the ICRC had to wade in with sticks, beating people into order, screaming, shouting, begging people to stay in line, to wait their turn.

These people had come through the parched, sun-burning bush, through the Renamo lines, through the minefields. They had come this far and they would do anything to survive. Desperation, one learns, is the beginning of life itself.

28

At the edge of the commotion, there was an empty grain bag lying in the hot dust. A child's feet were sticking out from underneath its ragged edge. Dave and I started filming this stark and haunting image of Mozambique's famine — this poignant, forgotten corpse of a child.

A woman was squatting at the head of the corpse, her head bowed down to the earth, her face hidden from the sun by a filthy wrap. She pulled the sack back away from the body. The child was still alive. He was naked and his shrivelled limbs were curled in a semi-foetal position. His large eyes were dull and lifeless and stared helplessly down at the dusty ground, while urine dribbled uncontrollably from his penis.

The woman looked up and said something to us, her eyes bright with anger. Then she leaned down and spoke harshly to her child. There was no response. Disgusted, she glared up at us, her eyes holding us with the intensity of her gaze. Finally, she threw the sack back over him again and looked away. Her eyes were filled with grief, but her movements were sharp and stiff with rage.

It was impossible to tell how much of her fury was directed at the government; at Renamo; at us with our shiny, intrusive cameras; and how much anger was directed at her son, for giving up the struggle to survive.

CHAPTER 5

THE KINDNESS OF STRANGERS

Angola. The place sums up all the heartbreak of Africa. A vast, beautiful, extremely rich country that lies shattered and filled with suffering and despair. Angola epitomises the dashed hopes, the senseless wars, the ruined economies that characterise so much of post-colonial Africa.

By the end of the anti-colonial war, three competing rebel organizations had emerged: the Popular Movement for the Liberation of Angola (MPLA) backed by the Soviet Union, the National Front for the Liberation of Angola (FNLA) supported by the US and China and the National Union for the total independence of Angola (UNITA) also funded by China, the US, Zaire and South Africa.

In 1974, after the coup in Lisbon when the new socialist government in Portugal had declared its intention to grant independence to its colonies, there had been exploratory power-sharing discussions between the three factions. But the talks rapidly broke down, and, in 1975, while the Portuguese were in the process of pulling out, it was obvious that there was no possibility of the three groups reaching a peaceful solution.

On November 11, 1975, the day the Portuguese flag was lowered in the capital Luanda, and the new flag of the independent People's Republic of Angola was raised in its stead, the sounds of gunfire from civil war were already echoing in the shanty towns on the outskirts of the city.

That war raged for seventeen years. The FNLA ceased to exist after a few months of the fighting, and the war was fought between the Soviet and Cuban-supported Marxist MPLA government and the Western-backed UNITA rebels. Since then, between nine and twenty million land mines have been planted in the country, over 500 000 people have been killed, and several thousand maimed. In addition, at the height of the war up to 1000 Angolans a day were dying from hunger and war-related diseases like cholera.

In 1991 there was a brief mirage of peace with the signing of an agreement between UNITA and the MPLA that would end the war and lead to multi-party elections in 1992.

The MPLA won, but only just. The UNITA leader Jonas Savimbi could not accept this result and in October 1992 street fighting broke out in the capital Luanda. After a week of heavy fighting in which over 4000 people were killed, Savimbi and his UNITA movement were driven out of the city and the 'new' war began. In the early stages of this war, the government forces were extremely hard-pressed to hang on to the territory they held because the numbers of troops they commanded had been seriously reduced by the demobilisation process agreed upon in the peace treaty and which UNITA had secretly ignored, giving them the upper hand when the fighting broke out again. Within a matter of weeks, most of Angola had become an ocean of chaos with the heavily besieged cities being mere islands of government control, and UNITA ranging freely across the countryside. For UNITA, having lost Luanda, the prize they now sought was Huambo in the south, Angola's second-largest city, deep in traditional UNITA territory, but for the moment still held by the government...

Cameraman Mark Chisholm of Reuters and I arrived in Luanda on Monday, February 22, 1993. It was an oppressively hot and humid day towards the end of the southern African rainy season; it was also the 46th day of fighting since the 'new' war had broken out.

After we cleared customs and immigration, someone from the UN offered to drive us to our hotel. We piled our luggage and TV equipment into the back of his 4x4 and climbed in after it. Crammed in awkwardly among our boxes and bags we set off towards the centre of the city. As we left the airport compound, my immediate impression of the city was of an average African capital: wide streets now rundown, shady avenues of exhausted lawns and tropical trees — flamboyants with surreal green leaves and bright scarlet flowers, huge spreading acacias, majestic jacarandas — the large paint-flaking billboards advertising soap and the local beer, the choking, noisy traffic hooting and roaring as it spasmed its way in irregular, illogical, bursts into the heart of the city.

But there was also the heat. The pressing, corrosive humidity from which, I soon learned, there was no escape. Every morning you woke to the pale dawn light and the first, soft clinging of the heat; from then on, every appointment you made had to be conducted in the sweltering mugginess, every physical movement, walking, filming, eating, was accomplished dripping in sweat. Your salt levels became depleted from constant perspiring and with that you lost your energy, and each day became a constant battle to do even the simplest, smallest things.

In Luanda, the heat, like the weariness that accompanies regret, was with you always.

But as we drove closer to the city centre, I began to see how horrible life in Luanda had become. The evidence of decay, war and neglect was everywhere: rusting hulks of cars and shipping containers littered the bare patches of red, sandy soil that were once parks; mounds of rotting garbage lay on the sidewalks; mini-lakes of raw sewerage in the potholes in the city streets that children were splashing around in — leading to massive outbreaks of cholera and malaria. The smell of it all was awful, mixing with the heat and leading to a foul miasma that hung over the city day and night.

I wrote in my diary that evening: 'Luanda is a cul-de-sac on the road to nowhere, a ruined city trapped in a time warp. Except for the vast, ridiculous, half-completed, Soviet-designed mausoleum to Augustinho Neto, nicknamed "the rocket", and a few ugly Cuban apartment blocks, nothing has been built since 1975 when the Portuguese left, and what remains is mostly falling apart. Filthy neon signs from the colonial days advertising beer and discos hang off the sides of buildings, there are still palm trees lining the "Marginal" — the road running around the beautiful bay (now filled with raw sewerage) but the tiny, hand-laid, black and white marble paving blocks have all long since been torn up, and the promenade is lined with rubbish and fallen lampposts.'

We drove down the *Avenida Ho Chi Minh* and turned left into the *Avenida Commandante Valodia*. The streets were filled with people — a constant stream of wretched humanity: hookers, beggars and hawkers with an almost ludicrous variety of goods for sale: cigarettes, underwear, handkerchiefs, wildly coloured rayon shirts, mock Ray-Bans, chromed Chinese wrench sets, Portuguese grammar books, inflatable Mickey Mouse dolls, Fanta beach balls, plastic bird cages with tiny flashing green and blue electric lights on the perches... the assortment was almost endless. No one could tell you how they got onto the streets; cigarettes and other staples were always there, but the waves of useless merchandise seemed to depend on what container had been looted in the port and the goods exchanged in return for diamonds, or arms, or medicines, or drugs.

The *Avenida Commandante Valodia* brought us to a huge litter-strewn plaza near the centre of the city. On a high marble plinth that had once borne the statue of a Portuguese conqueror stood a rusting South African armoured car, its rubber wheels flat and rotting on their rims. Behind it stood a large cutout billboard of a blue and white peace dove — a sad reminder of the brief months of Angola's peace.

Beyond the plaza lay the Hotel Tivoli on the *Rua de Missao*. It was a $175.00-a-night air-conditioned oasis from the Dantesque horror of Luanda's streets. The foyer gleamed with modern, freshly-scrubbed tiles, and a fountain with goldfish in the tiny square pond tinkled near the bar that served ice-cold beer and sodas. Mark and I checked in and then went to the offices of the World Food Programme (WFP) to find out about the possibility of hitching a ride on food aid flights to the stricken cities of Angola.

Fritz was in charge of allocating flights to the press. A German citizen born in the Belgian Congo, as a young boy in

World War II he and his family had escaped to neutral Portuguese Angola in a dugout canoe across the Congo River. He had gone to school in Luanda and learned to speak Portuguese. He was a colourful character who simply described himself as 'of the continent'. His life backed up this claim: he owned a house in Johannesburg, and in his adult life he had, among other picaresque experiences, spent time in jail in Marxist Mozambique, and now he was back in Angola, working for the UN. Over tiny cups of thick dark espresso in his (air-conditioned) office, Fritz introduced us to the confusing melange of observed fact and unconfirmed rumour that often is the closest thing one can get to an eyewitness account of the war in Angola.

'Four thousand people were killed in the battle for Luanda,' Fritz told us. 'It started at about two o'clock in the morning. I woke up to the loudest shooting I have ever heard. UNITA attacked five places simultaneously: the port, the main police station, the television station, the Ministry of Foreign Affairs and the Ministry of the Interior. UNITA started the fight and it continued the whole weekend. All the UNITA hierarchy were based in the Hotel Turismo. The government attacked the hotel and it took three-quarters of an hour to kill them all. With my own eyes I saw civilians throwing a UNITA guy out the window of a tall building. I also saw ten of them being put in a pile in a public square. Tyres were put around their necks and they were burnt alive. They say that three thousand UNITA were killed altogether. The rest of them managed to fight their way to Caxito, about 60 kilometres north of the city, and they are there still. They plan to attack all the supply points: the water, gasoline, electricity. They hit the water regularly, and we are expecting them to come for the gasoline. There are only six and a half days of fuel left in the city. We know that there are hundreds of them that have infiltrated the city and are just waiting for the right time. And the others will come, make no mistake, even if only for revenge. They'll come in up through the sewers, and strike when the time is right.'

That night, as I lay in bed I heard gunfire — the unmistakable rapid pneumatic thud of an AK-47 on the streets nearby and, then, just as suddenly, an answering crackle. It died away quickly and, with my heart beating, I opened the window out of my perverse curiosity and peered out. But there was nothing except silence and the unclean smell of the city rising through the muggy darkness.

Fritz probably exaggerated some of the details in his stories, but I understood his mode of discourse. I had only been in Angola for one night and already I was beginning to believe in the sewers.

The next morning when I woke I went into the bathroom and turned on the tap. It coughed and spluttered and a thick brown sludge trickled out of the spout and then stopped. At breakfast, we heard reports that UNITA had shelled the pumping station. In this case the story was quite likely to be true, but, at the same time, try as we might, we could get no independent verification of these claims. The story took on a life of its own as it ebbed and flowed through the streets and ruined buildings of Luanda along with the black market cigarettes and the plastic bird cages. We tried to get a statement from the Ministry of Defence but there was, we were told, no one available to speak to us.

The kwanza is the name of the currency in Angola. At the beginning of 1993, one American dollar was worth 26000 kwanzas and inflation was running at well over 1000%. For some reason, it was mostly women who did the dirty work in the illegal currency deals that seemed to run Luanda's economy. All over the city you could see women with bored expressions on their faces standing on street corners waving Bible-sized wads of kwanzas in the air. Technically, they were breaking the law, but nobody, least of all the police, seemed to care. We stopped at one corner and handed the woman a $100.00 bill. She scrutinised it carefully, shook her head and handed it back.

'What's wrong?' Mark demanded.

'It's a 1988 bill,' our driver told us. 'Nobody in Luanda will accept them. There are too many 1988 bills that are forged.' Fortunately, we had some others — and most of them were dated 1990. $100 bills dated 1988, these had now joined the pantheon of Luanda's extensive urban mythology. Not even the government-run airlines would take them. Later, at the airport when I had to pay an excess baggage charge, I watched a man run my $100 dollar bill through a certified US Currency Verifier, and then, after it had passed the test, hold it up to check the date. Luckily, I knew better than to even think of using a 1988 bill. I also knew better than to bother questioning his method. By then, I had learned that, having known only this war for over twenty years, for Angolans nothing could be taken at face value any more.

Fritz had agreed to accompany us, and another journalist, Andy Meldrum, a free-lancer from Harare, for the morning. First he was to take us to a UN-sponsored refugee camp on the outskirts of Luanda. To get there we had to pass a huge open-air market on the edge of Luanda bay. The market was called *Roque Santeiro* and was named after a popular Brazilian soap opera. Neither Mark nor I had ever seen anything quite like it. It was about four or five kilometres long and perhaps a kilometre wide and the whole of it had once been a rubbish dump, so the smell was horrific. Thousands of tiny makeshift stalls had been set up amidst the rotting piles of garbage, and streams of people wandered in amongst them buying and selling almost anything you could think of: cheap plastic combs, beer, colddrinks, medicines, mineral water, tyres, socks, tins of bully beef, shoes, exercise books, peanuts, whiskey, car parts, aid grain in fifty-kilogram sacks clearly marked *Not For Resale,* condoms, stereo systems... There was almost certainly a greater variety of goods available for sale at *Roque Santeiro* than at an average shopping mall anywhere in the Western world. Of course, drugs like heroin and cocaine were easily available, and it was said that you could buy AK-47s and other weapons, like land mines and hand grenades, deep in the centre aisles of *Roque Santeiro.*

On our way back from the refugee camp, we stopped on the side of the road to film the market. We set up the camera and the tripod and Mark had just squeezed off a few shots when the local police arrived on the scene. Did we, they wanted to know, have permission to film the market?

We showed them our Angolan press cards. Of course, they were not good enough. We needed specific permission to film the market, specific *written* permission.

From the beginning of the encounter, Mark refused to allow himself to be bullied. 'One thing I can tell you right now,' he muttered under his breath to me. 'They're not taking this fucking tape.' Having made his position clear, Mark, a highly experienced cameraman and a veteran of Bosnia and a number of other wars, retreated behind his tripod and stood glowering over the top of his camera at the policemen. The policemen glared back.

Andy and I kept silent, both of us also having been in similar situations before, and both of us trying to sum up whether it was better, in this particular case, to be aggressive or conciliatory. Anyway, at this point, we were fairly confident that Fritz with his fluent Portuguese and, more importantly, his UN identity card would be able to smooth the situation over and we would soon be on our way. Fritz got out of his 4x4 and came over to where the policemen and we were having our stand off. An officer demanded his identity card. Fritz took it out of his shirt pocket and the officer grabbed it rudely out of his hand. He turned to Andy and me and demanded our cards. At first, we refused to hand them over. We couldn't understand exactly what was being said, but Fritz looked worried. 'Don't play games with them,' he told us. We handed the officer our press cards. He grabbed them equally rudely. He motioned for all of us to follow him.

We set off towards the police station, just a little way down the road. It was an old colonial building with curved red roof tiles and the cracked, dirty remains of blue and white porcelain tiles on the interior finishes. It was set in the middle of a hot, dusty compound littered with bones and broken glass. They marched us — Andy and me, and Fritz, in front, Mark dragging his feet in the rear and clutching his camera, around the side of the main building. At the back of the building was a large, almost leafless tree with remains of the white paint to keep termites from eating its bark still visible around the base. Underneath the tree stood a policeman with a metre-long length of rubber hose doubled up in his right hand. In front of him were three teenage boys, stripped down to their waists, sweating profusely, and jogging in erratic circles around the trunk. Every time one of them passed the point where the policeman was standing, he would lash out viciously at the boy with his rubber hose, and the boy would scream as the blow raised another thick weal on the skin of his back. What the boys had done to deserve this torture we didn't dare ask.

Andy turned to me and muttered under his breath: 'I think we're next.'

Fritz was not amused. 'Don't joke with these people,' he whispered.

'These fuckers can do what they like,' Mark mumbled furiously. 'But I promise you they're not getting this tape.'

We were ushered across the square, past the tree (the policeman stopped beating them for a moment to watch us file past) and into the office of the *commandante.* The room was, for a station commander's office, somewhat oddly furnished. A colour portable TV set and video recorder took up pride of place on the wall alongside the door. A gold-coloured plastic clock in the shape of a peacock adorned the wall opposite, and the floor was covered in a garish ruby-tinted carpet. A gleaming AK-47 stood in one corner next to a filing cabinet, and a plastic-covered lounge suite took up whatever other space was available. The *commandante* himself sat behind a large steel desk, and, just above his head, a Fanta beach ball was dangling from a long string tacked to the ceiling.

He motioned for us to sit down. The officer who had arrested us stepped forward and put our identity cards down on the desk in front of him. The *commandante* squinted down at them briefly, and then looked up at Fritz who had launched into a long and apologetic speech, which was clearly the right thing to do under the circumstances. I could only understand two or three out of every ten words, so I gave up trying to follow the conversation, and instead concentrated on watching the beach ball sway and spin slowly in the wind over the *commandante*'s head. The window of the *commandante*'s office was open and, as Fritz explained and re-explained what exactly we had been doing, the screams of the unfortunate boys drifted through the window towards us.

Finally, Fritz was finished. He had obviously said the right things, and the *commandante* got up from behind his desk and handed us our identity cards. After thanking him in our rudimentary Portuguese, we shook hands with him and stepped outside again.

The beating had stopped. The tree stood forlornly at the edge of the square in the baking sun. The boys and their tormentor were gone. The only sign of what had happened was the length of rubber hose that lay abandoned in the dust beneath the tree.

We had dinner that night with another Reuters colleague, Judith Matloff, who was based temporarily in Luanda, and an American diplomat whom I shall call Andy. We went to a Chinese restaurant on the long, thin peninsula that formed the large natural harbour of Luanda bay. We ordered soup and lobster and sat crowded around one of the tiny tables in the packed restaurant. Every journalist in Angola wanted to get to Huambo, or as close to it as possible. At that point, there were no WFP aid flights going in, and the Angolan military responded with stunning silence to our frequent requests for some sort of press facility. Some journalists were trying to get to Huambo through the old UNITA contacts in Johannesburg, but with the changes in South Africa those relationships had become strained, and they weren't meeting with much success either.

Hundreds of people were dying daily in the fighting for Huambo, but nobody could get any real, confirmed details about the progress of the battle. The only source of facts were the garbled, terrified accounts from the refugees who were streaming across southern Angola in their thousands. But many of them had left Huambo a week or ten days before.

Their reports were not only old, but they were filled with the contradictions and unverifiable claims of people anywhere who witness the tiny fragments of terror and mayhem that accompany war. In the end, without proper sources of information, the only picture that was emerging from Huambo was a kaleidoscope of confusion. *Angola War without Witness* had become the clichéd headline for a number of articles, but, like all clichés, it emerged out of a solid reality. The war here was awful — the agony of Luanda itself confirmed that — but there was no way of reporting on the reality of the war, one could only scratch around the periphery of the conflict: one could wander among the living ghosts of the war: the tens of thousands of refugees, the maimed, the wounded, the outbreaks of cholera among the children, the ever-present hunger, the shattered buildings and infrastructure, the bizarre, barely-functioning economy. But the hard questions — Who was winning?, Who was losing? What was actually happening? — they were impossible to find answers to. The war was invisible; it was only the rumours that were real.

It was with this in mind that we asked Andy about Huambo at dinner.

He smiled. 'Why don't you tell me what's going on?'

'But your spy satellites,' I protested. 'Don't they tell you what's going on?'

'They tell us some things,' he said, slowly. 'Some of which I can tell you, and some of which I can't. The one thing I can tell you is that Huambo is the worst battle on the planet, and has been since the Gulf War.'

'What about Bosnia?' Mark asked.

'Bosnia's bad. But Huambo is worse, much worse.'

'That's why we need to go there,' Judith said. 'How else is the world going to know?'

Andy leant forward and picked up his mug of beer. 'You tell the government here that, and then let me know what they say.'

'But can't you maybe swing something for us?'

'No way,' Andy shook his head. 'Our influence is limited with them. And, anyway, it's too dangerous. The government is hanging on by the skin of its teeth there. From what we can judge, they still hold the governor's palace and one or two streets around it. That's it. They can't even get military helicopters in there to supply their own troops. The last time they tried, UNITA shot one down and the other just managed to get out.

'No one can get in or out of Huambo until the fighting stops. Until either UNITA takes it or the government drives them back.'

'What do you suggest we do then?'

'Wait, like everyone else.'

'But we can't wait forever.'

'What other options do you have?'

That evening CNN was broadcasting wall-to-wall live coverage from New York city. A terrorist bomb had been set off in the World Trade Centre. Six people were killed in the explosion.

'If we have a flight to Huambo,' Fritz told us the next morning, 'I promise to do my best to get you on it. But, we don't have one, and I can tell you we won't have one until two weeks after the fighting has stopped. I can get you on a flight to Malange, Luena, Lubango, even maybe Mbanza-Congo, but forget about Huambo...'

Clearly, if we were going to achieve anything in Angola we needed an Angolan fixer. Later that morning at the press centre, Judith introduced us to Teresa Costa. Teresa was a large, jovial woman who brooked no nonsense from anyone. As a fixer, she was an invaluable mine of information and contacts but, more importantly, she also opened up Angola and the Angolans to me in a way that I simply hadn't expected.

Her first task was to take us to Cacuaco. We needed some images of the war. At the least, some pictures of soldiers and tanks and other military hardware. We accepted that, for the moment, we couldn't get to Huambo, but it was ridiculous to be covering a civil war and have no shots of anything remotely resembling military activity.

Cacuaco was the pumping station for Luanda's water supply, which, we were told, had been attacked a few days before. It was also on the road to Caxito which UNITA held and was the nearest front line of the fighting to Luanda.

The road to Cacuaco took us past the traffic-choked section around *Roque Santeiro* and then out beyond the city and along the coast. Once, it must have been a beautiful road and, here and there, one could still catch glimpses of what it must have once been like: a grove of tall coconut palms waving in the wind against the backdrop of the blue sea, a red-tiled cottage with a deep shady verandah and faded blue walls now thick with dirt and grime, a stream meandering through the countryside dotted with deep pools and banks of reeds.

But this once picturesque countryside was now a moonscape of decay. Old, untilled fields were littered with rubbish and car wrecks, a few baobab trees and the odd prickly pear bush, shrivelled in the heat, were the only things growing in the red, bone-dry soil. Hundreds of people lined the road, trying to sell horrible-smelling, dried fish blackened from the sun and covered in swarms of flies; tiny bags of wrinkled, undernourished peanuts; bottles of palm wine or cans of Fanta, Coke, Sprite and Castle Beer — all from South Africa.

Many of the people were refugees from the UNITA occupation of Caxito. There was no room for them in Luanda itself, and there was nothing for them to do here, on the outskirts, except let the war swirl on around them and try to scratch out some type of existence from the pathetic means available to them. As we drove by in the battered, rented Ford XR-3 that Teresa had arranged for us, the people held up their pitiful wares in hope that we would stop and buy something, anything just to bring a few kwanza with which they could buy some stolen aid grain or perhaps some bananas. It was a shocking journey, that short trip to Cacuaco. For here, in the countryside, one saw the real meaning of the devastation of Angola, the real destruction and despair that twenty years of war had brought. Here, too, far more than in Luanda, one could sense the fear that underlay daily life in Angola. Everything these people did, every morning they woke up, every time they stepped into their fields or took up their places on the edge of the road, and every night they lay down to sleep, was punctuated by the knowledge that UNITA was only a few kilometres away on one side and the MPLA only a few kilometres away on the other — at almost any moment they could find themselves in the middle of a hail of shrapnel, or, more commonly, they could step on a land mine planted by one side or the other...

Chaos reigned at the pumping station on the river Zenza. The immediate area around the pump was churned up into a huge field of mud with foot-deep potholes lying just beneath the black surface. The pumping station itself could do nothing to supply the areas of the city where the pipes had long since broken, so there was a fleet of decrepit water tankers that came to the banks of the river daily to fetch water to take back to the stricken suburbs.

The narrow road served both for transporting the water to the city and for ferrying troops and equipment to the front line near Caxito, and there was a constant snarl-up of water lorries and tanks and troop-carriers on their way to the front.

A small concrete bridge spanned the river. There was a pair of palm trees that stood next to it, and a Russian tank stood guard on the other side. It was manned by young Angolan soldiers who were scarcely more than boys. The Cold War days of foreign troops and observers were over. The world had pulled out and left the Angolans to fight it out among themselves in their 'new' war.

We drove up to the bridge, Teresa confidently behind the wheel. A soldier came up to speak to us. This was as far as we were allowed to go. UNITA was only fifteen kilometres away, from this point on was *uma zona militar*. We turned around and parked the car a little way away, and came back to the bridge with the camera and tripod.

There was no question of filming here without permission, even Mark conceded that much. The two of us stood to one side trying to look as inconspicuous as possible while Teresa went to negotiate with the soldier who had stopped us in the first place. He was a non-commissioned officer of some type, probably a sergeant, so it was conceivable that he could give us the go-ahead to film. While we were waiting for Teresa to conclude the negotiations, a very young soldier, probably no more than sixteen years old, came up to speak to us. He had a friendly smile and his gun was swung nonchalantly over his shoulder. He was wearing good boots, the new FAA (*Forcas Armadas Angolano* that, in terms of the peace agreement was supposed to have been an amalgamation of both the MPLA and UNITA to form the new Angolan defence force but was now basically MPLA) camouflage pattern combat fatigues, and a black tank top that was stretched tight over his muscular young torso. He was also stoned out of his mind on drugs — probably marijuana. I offered him a cigarette. He put it in the pocket of his fatigues and grinned vacantly back at me.

'*Tu conheces Rambo?*' he asked.

'*Si.*'

He pointed to the centre of his chest. '*Eu sou como Rambo um artista de guerra*' — I am like Rambo, an artist of war.

Not being quite sure what he expected as a response to this revelation, I nodded and smiled politely at him. Also, my Portuguese was not up to continuing the conversation much longer. He seemed satisfied, though, and swaggered back across the bridge, his AK-47 still swung over his shoulder.

Teresa came back and told us that the NCO had given us permission to film — only the pumping operations, nothing to do with the military or the bridge. Mark put the camera on the tripod and started filming the tankers taking on water. Teresa and I stood back, well out of shot and chatted while I took a few notes on things she was telling me about life in Luanda.

Suddenly, an Angolan officer, fairly senior judging by the amount of gold braid on his shoulder, burst in screaming at Mark and, through agitated gestures, indicated that he had to stop filming. Teresa and I rushed over to where Mark was and Teresa started trying to explain. The man was apoplectic. He was standing right next to us and screaming at the hapless NCO (who looked very frightened) a short distance away and then turning back to our group and screaming at the three of us. Mark and I were silent, but Teresa refused to back down;

she was trying to interrupt the tirade to get a word in edgewise.

While all this pandemonium was going on, the young soldier who I had spoken to earlier pushed his way between us, and shoved the barrel of his AK-47 just a few inches under the officer's chin. The boy stood there and shouted at the officer. In his drug-befuddled brain, he was protecting us, and perhaps standing up for his NCO against an officer who he seemed not to know.

Up until that point the situation had been mildly amusing. But, now, it became downright frightening. The young Rambo stood there with his finger on the trigger, swaying slightly back and forth on his heels, shouting aggressively at the officer.

The officer grabbed the barrel of the gun and pushed it away from his head. Then, still holding it firmly in one hand, he used the other to try and push the soldier's finger through the trigger guard off the trigger. The soldier shouted at him and pushed back at the officer. The two of them started wrestling for possession of the gun. Their feet were slipping in the mud and the barrel was waving in all directions, including ours. Slowly, millimetre by millimetre, we watched as the two of them struggled back and forth for control. Finally, the officer managed to push the boy's finger off the trigger. He jerked the gun violently out of the boy's hands. The boy stumbled back slightly, and the officer punched him, hard, in the chest. The boy tried to stand his ground, but the officer hit him again, deflecting the blow onto the shoulder. The NCO came up and led the soldier away, slapping him on the back of the head as they went.

Now it was our turn. The officer handed the gun to a soldier standing nearby and started berating Teresa again. But the force had gone out of his anger. She calmed him down easily, and he stood there listening to her explain. Finally, he nodded his head in agreement. He stepped over to Mark and, taking him completely by surprise, embraced him in the Latin way, putting his head first to the left of Mark's utterly bemused and deeply Anglo-Saxon face, and then to the right of it. Then he grabbed me and repeated the same performance. He nodded and waved briskly as the three of us climbed into the car and drove gratefully off.

'What did you tell him?' I asked Teresa when we were a little way down the road.

'I told him you were friends of Angola. That by filming our water problems, you were showing the rest of the world how we are suffering.'

None of us said much on the desperately crowded, littered, despairing road back to Luanda. Just outside the city, we passed what had, until fairly recently, been an old Cuban army base. The perimeter was surrounded by rusting barbed wire and, inside, a few battered APCs stood up on blocks bleeding dirty oil into the dry earth. Outside the barracks where the men had slept there was a small concrete wall with a faded blue and white striped Cuban flag painted on its surface.

Had things changed much, I wanted to know, now that Angola had given up communism.

Teresa roared with laughter behind the wheel. 'Angola was never a communist country. It was a surrealistic country.'

The war stopped at sunset on a Friday. Or, at least, in Luanda it seemed to. As the light grew soft and golden and the shadows lengthened across the ruined boulevards, a kind of peace fell over the city. The government ministries high up on the hill were closed. One assumed that, somehow, communications were received, orders given and troops moved around the country, but there was never any sign of movement from within the government compounds – and certainly no chance whatsoever of any kind of statement for the press.

The stores closed and the streets became cooler and filled with deep, angular shadows where old men lazed on chairs and children skipped rope and played hopscotch. Without the frenetic activity of the week time, the city took on all the clichéd torpor of the tropics. One began to notice things like the thick green vine growing over a shaded balcony, or the people sitting at the pavement café, the plastic chairs and tables precariously balanced on the broken paving stones, the patrons sipping beer and ignoring the smells and noise of the streets, a faded blue or pink shutter hanging askance on its hinges above a crumbling stone windowsill, the bay still and limpid as a mirror — a bird cutting across the horizon and the palms gently silhouetted against the sky slowly turning pink...

At these moments, it was impossible not to find something both tragic and magnificent about Luanda. The dead colonial splendour was grieved for only in places like Lisbon, Madeira and the razor-wire suburbs of Johannesburg. It was the present, not the past, that one mourned in Luanda. Two decades of war had merged the two into one, terrible, inescapable mode of existence. You understood the bitterness that goes with twenty years of picking your way through the ruins of a once-beautiful city and daily wondering what might have been, and yet you knew also that the glimpses of beauty, and peace, were as real and as tangible as the sadness, and that they would haunt your memory forever.

On Saturday morning Teresa took us to film at an old mansion that had stood in Luanda for about 300 years. The large entrance hall was cool and gloomy inside. A wide stone staircase, half-moons worn into its treads from years of being tramped on, curved up into the darkness of the second storey beneath a Renaissance-style archway. Barefoot people, the poorest of Luanda's poor, wandered up and down in the semi-darkness going about their business and talking quietly among themselves.

The walls were covered in filth and graffiti and in most places the plaster had fallen away exposing the mix of sand and lime that held the two-foot thick walls together. Here and there, one would see a bleached seashell or smooth round pebble mixed in with the ancient mortar. The decay of the building was so complete that it was impossible to tell the difference between which was simply from centuries of use, and which was a result of Luanda's more recent disintegration.

We climbed the stone steps onto a mouldering wooden staircase that in places had rotted so badly that we could see the floor beneath us through the holes in the wood. Ragged children leaped up and down the rickety steps that seemed that they would come crashing down at any minute.

On the second storey the rooms were divided up into tiny compartments in which sometimes whole families lived. The partitions were made of a variety of cast-off materials: dirty cardboard, old sacks strung up on wire, rusty sheets of tin — anything that was available. The little rooms themselves were spotlessly clean and tidy. In one a kitten was lying on a makeshift bed (neatly made up) cleaning itself; in another, a schoolgirl with her hair in plaits and the chewed stub of a pencil in her hand was poring over a worn exercise book while her mother prepared lunch over a small coal brazier; yet another was empty, but the sun shone through the dirty fragments of a window and fell on a tiny collection of house plants in glass jars on the floor.

The combination of squalor and pride seemed to epitomise Luanda, and we took a lot of footage inside this ruined hulk of a building. When we had finished we stepped out into the blazing sun on the potholed street outside. I noticed that the front of the house was built up well above the street level with a stone staircase leading up to the front entrance way. Just below the top of the staircase was a pair of rusty steel rings set into the stone.

Teresa saw me looking at them. 'This house used to belong to the richest woman in Luanda. That wall was once the edge of the bay, the water came up right up to it. Those big rings were for tying boats onto,' she told me.

And how, I wanted to know, did this woman become so rich?

'She was a slave dealer,' Teresa said.

On Sunday, like everybody else, we went out to the Ilha. The streets on Sunday were completely empty, with just the ever-present streams of beggar children rooting in the piles of garbage for something to eat or sell, and the sun shining out of a cloudless blue sky filling the silence and the emptiness of the city with a dead white heat.

The Ilha was crowded with people enjoying the sunshine and the cold, green Atlantic crashing against the white sands of the beach. The road running down the centre of the narrow peninsula was the only street in the city jam-packed with traffic. A shanty town had sprung up all along the edge of the road and there were people trying to sell the usual bizarre array of things like cigarettes, baby clothes and dried fish. The restaurants were crammed with aid workers and the members of the affluent Angolan elite while the *povo* struggled and sweated and begged in the street outside. I noticed a gleaming black Lotus Turbo Esprit edging its way forward through the traffic and around the potholes in fits and starts like a shark confronting an uneven current, forced alternately to slow down and then roar forward a few frustrating metres.

We sat down at an outside restaurant directly on the beach and ordered prawns and a bottle of cold white wine. Just a little way off there were young men and women playing in the surf, their gorgeous bodies gleaming with wetness and straining against the tightness of their skimpy day-glo swimsuits. There was a fence around the eating area to keep the *povo* out, but children came and pressed their noses to the wire mesh and stared at the plates of prawns and seafood being brought to the tables.

Suddenly, out of nowhere, came the heart-stopping, gut-wrenching, earth-shattering boom of a MiG fighter-bomber screaming low over the beach and breaking the sound barrier just a hundred metres or so above us. There was an instant of sheer terror that made your heart thump like an animal in your chest and adrenalin surge through your veins leaving you trembling and exhausted for minutes afterwards. The plane had disappeared over the horizon in the space of time it took your heart to spasm once in panic, but it left you knowing something of what that sound must be like for the UNITA soldiers huddling in the burning sun in the trenches around Caxito, waiting for the bombs and rockets that blazed off the MiG's wings and turned the hot, red dust into blood and fragments of human flesh.

And when the prawns and wine were finished and the children had stopped staring at you and you went back to the hotel and took the lift up to the top floor, you could see the plumes of black smoke on the distant horizon. The war was that close.

On Monday morning Teresa and Mark and I took the potholed, overcrowded road heading out of Luanda past the all-important water pipeline to the city, past the old Portuguese army base that once saw a mutiny by the ANC's Umkhonto We Sizwe and was now occupied by the Angolan army. The concrete barracks were painted a bright pink that was almost surreal amidst the all the squalor surrounding it. We drove past the twisted, rusting railway tracks with weeds growing up through the sleepers, through the arid plains on the outskirts of the city, through what were once peaceful suburbs and abundant fields of mango and cashew trees.

About forty minutes down the road, we came to an abandoned truck stop motel and garage called *Montesclaros* — Mountain View. The windows and doors of the motel had long since been smashed and removed, the walls were black with grease and filth, and the workshops stood empty, stripped of tools.

We stopped and dozens of crippled and legless people, mostly men, came pouring out from the gaping holes in the building. They hobbled over to us on crutches and flimsy, pathetic wheelchairs and swarmed around us, begging for money, food or drink. Some were almost blind from the battery-acid moonshine they made themselves, most were toothless from malnutrition, and all of them were hideously scarred and deformed in some way.

They were the *mutilados* — the mutilated ones. The human wreckage of Angola's civil war. Most of them were ex-soliders, crippled by land mines, and dependent on a tiny pension from the government to support them and their families. It was a horrible place, this *Montesclaros,* a place where men, still in their twenties, rotted their lives away. There was no hope left for them and their families. Their brains and wills had withered from anger and battery acid. They were the detritus of a society that could no longer function, a society which had used their bodies to fight its war and then had abandoned them.

Teresa took us inside to where the old hotel rooms were crammed with these broken men, living among the stench of piss and shit and decades of accumulated filth.

Journalists have to interview people, so, with Teresa translating we asked some of them to tell us their stories. The first man we spoke to was too drunk to make sense, he simply rocked backwards and forwards on his crutches, drooling down his chin and staring at us with wild, reddened eyes in the semi-darkness. Antonio Goncalves was the next man. He was willing to speak: 'It is because of the war that the government can do nothing to help us. It is Savimbi who is to blame. He wants this war. It is him who is making us suffer.'

Elias Job was hunched up in a wheelchair in a dark corner of the building that reeked of urine. Yes, he said, in a quiet voice that one could hardly hear, he would speak to us. I handed the microphone to Teresa who translated what he told us. 'When the fighting broke out again, my wife and children were in Huambo. I have not heard from them in months now. I have no idea where they are, even if they are alive.' Elias paused, looking at us with clear simple stare — a look without excessive emotion or self-pity, the look of a man who has a simple truth to share with the world: 'There is nothing to look forward to now,' he told us. 'I would rather die than continue living in this hell.'

Teresa stood up and handed the microphone back to me. 'Please,' she said, wiping the tears from her eyes. 'No more questions. I cannot stand to hear any more.'

As we were leaving, there was an uproar among the men over something, a handmade knife flashed up from its hiding place in the seat of a wheelchair, and a man on crutches swung around and fled, with the man in the wheelchair chasing him across the littered tarmac. Suddenly there was chaos, swirling all around us. We got in the car and they were still fighting amongst themselves as we drove off.

Our destination was further down the road, a place where there was hope. It was the Red Cross centre in Viana where Dutch Red Cross workers were training Angolans to make prostheses and in physiotherapy techniques for amputees. Angola has the highest number of amputees in the world, an estimated 40 000 − 60 000 people, but the real number is probably much higher as many of the injured in Angola's war either bled to death in the remote bush or were never able to reach the cities for treatment and counting. The country is filled with an immense population of suffering, crippled people. There must be a hundred *Montesclaros* in Angola. But Viana was different, it was an island of hope amidst the despair. It was a place where Angolans were being helped and, at the same time, helping themselves.

We got out of the car and stepped into the bright sunlight. There were neat lawns and flower beds blooming next to the parking lot. The centre itself was a collection of spotlessly clean and simple prefab sheds. Here the men were also all crippled by land mines. But here they were quiet and subdued, smoking cigarettes in the shade of the prefab houses. Bounding over the parking lot towards us was a small boy, perhaps six or seven years old. He was on crutches too. His right leg had been amputated from above the knee. He was amazingly agile on his crutches, moving towards us with a light, easy rhythm and pushing a toy lorry made of wire and cans.

The Red Cross people introduced us. The little boy's name was Chico. He smiled shyly when we spoke to him and sometimes half-hid his face in the collar of his worn, but clean shirt. He didn't speak English and we didn't speak more than a few words of Portuguese, but we managed to exchange a few childish pleasantries with him before we moved on to do our main work, which was to film the prostheses centre, the physiotherapy ward, and interview some patients and the Red Cross workers.

Chico was waiting for us when we were finished. He was standing near the parking lot on his crutches, moving his wire lorry up and down in an arc along the hot gravel surface. He didn't say much, he just stood there alone, the only child in this hospital. The Red Cross people told us his story − as far as they could piece it together. He used to live with his parents in Uige, far to the north of Luanda. Chico himself was not quite sure what happened. He knew he stepped on a land mine, but where his parents were, he could not say. And when we asked how he got to Viana he shrugged his skinny shoulders and looked away.

Chico had survived through a combination of luck and the kindness of strangers. There must have been a hundred thousand orphans like Chico in Angola. I had already seen scores of them on the streets of Luanda, and I was going to see them all over the country in Luena, Malange, Cubal, Benguela... Chico's story was sad, desperately sad, but his was only one of many stories just like it.

Before we left, I bent down to inspect his lorry. It was skilfully made, with the wire body symmetrical and the bits of tin for the wheels and mirrors and the front grille cut and shaped neatly. I told him how good I thought it was, and teasingly asked him if he wanted to sell it. Chico smiled and half-hid his face. No, he told me, he wanted to keep it.

We climbed in the car and headed back for Luanda. Chico was still waving at us as we drove out the gate of the Red Cross compound. His small arm high in the air, his free crutch leaning against his chest, his one leg and the other crutch planting him firmly on the ground.

Daybreak was orange and red over the horizon. The hulks of the planes parked on the tarmac were silhouetted like giant black insects against the sky. The engines of the WFP Antonov screamed and the exhausts blew a scalding rush of half-burned avgas over us in the dawn coolness. We couldn't hear ourselves speak above the roar of the engines, but the Russian pilot wearing the bright green shorts, dirty T-shirt and white, hairless legs stuck into cheap shiny leather shoes without socks motioned frantically for us to get aboard. He smiled at us with a full set of gold incisors as we climbed up the ramp at the back of the plane and found a seat for ourselves among the pile of grain sacks. The ramp came up, shutting the new daylight out of the hold, and clanging shut with a straining and clanking of gears and steel joins fitting uncertainly.

Outside the hold the roar of the engines turned into a loud screaming whine and through the scratched portholes we could see the airport buildings turn and disappear as the plane taxied onto the runway. We gathered speed past the wreckage of old Cold War East Bloc war material: the crushed skeletons of fighter planes, tanks, troop trucks, radar dishes, shell cases, rusting anti-aircraft guns — all of it piled up on the edge of the runway, a mute testimony to Angola's ruined past and even worse present that stubbornly refused to turn itself into a future for the country.

With a final whine of the engines and a windmilling of arms and legs as the acceleration pulled us haphazardly around the maize bags in the hold we took off into the air above Luanda. Mark and I were heading for Luena where the WFP was running a feeding scheme. Luena was once an important stop on what had been the strategically and economically vital Benguela railway that ran south-central Africa's goods from the landlocked interior to the deep-water Atlantic Ocean ports of Benguela and Lobito. The railway had ceased to run years ago and government-held Luena now was an isolated town in the deep eastern wilderness of Angola. Luena was completely surrounded by UNITA, and heavily-besieged. A town that had been built for a few thousand people was choked with over 30 000 refugees. Until a few weeks before, UNITA had held many of the streets on the edge of town. Heavy fighting had driven them back, but only a couple of kilometres into the bush. In some areas they were only hundreds of metres away from the edge of town. It was at night, we were told, that most of the fighting took place.

We flew over Luena at over 10 000 feet, and then the pilot banked sharply in the air and we started a tight downward run. With the engines screaming and the G-forces popping our eyes, pulling the loose flesh on our faces downwards and seeming to drag the contents of our guts through our asses, we spiralled rapidly down towards the runway. The diameter of each turn was as small as possible to reduce the risk of passing over the UNITA lines and their loosing off an RPG, or even a few stray bullets, in our direction. The ground below and the blue sky above flashed alternately past the porthole like a bad video effect, and suddenly there was teeth-juddering bump, and a screech as the tyres smoked on the runway. The engines howled and the wings shuddered as the pilot slowed the plane on the tarmac.

While he was still taxiing, the ramp was already being lowered, and within seconds of the pilot bringing the plane to a stop, a truck appeared in the gap of daylight and a crowd of ragged men swarmed into the hold and started dragging the grain sacks out and loading them onto the back of the truck.

We made our way down the ramp and jumped out onto the runway. Here, at last, was the edge of the invisible war, the point at which the rumours began and from here flowed inwards towards the capital. There were two Soviet helicopters parked nearby covered in a thick layer of oil and dust. The runway was surrounded by government troops, mostly the blue-uniformed 'police' who were, in reality, soldiers hastily transformed into policemen and who were the MPLA's answer to UNITA's refusal to demob their troops. They were mostly young men and teenage boys, but they had the toughness and the determined look of battle-hardened frontline troops. They were lean and grim-faced; their AK-47s were clean and oiled and hung comfortably on their shoulders; their eyes were fierce and arrogant, but their hands were calm and their fingers hung lazily and confidently over the steel workings of their rifles.

We took a UN jeep into town. Every single building had been hit by ordnance. Every wall was pockmarked with bullet holes and most buildings had taken worse hits from mortars and rocket grenades that left gaping holes of rubble everywhere. Tens of thousands of refugees had fled into the town. Everywhere you looked, ragged people were living. They were crammed into the railway station, into dirty, windowless buildings that had once been schools, hotels or shops; many of them were living on the streets, cooking their meagre portions of maize on the sidewalks and sleeping in amongst the fallen lampposts and mortar shell holes.

A detachment of 'Ninjas' was based in Luena. They were the elite police guard who wore blue overalls and black berets. Many of them also wore black leather jackets or black bullet-proof vests. It was the look and the image of these vests and berets, and the mirror sunglasses that made their eyes invisible, that had given them their name. The Ninjas had a fearsome reputation in combat and their presence here showed how seriously the government was taking the fight for Luena.

We drove to the military hospital, past the corpse of a dead dog lying in the middle of the road hideously bloated and stinking, its hair and skin a mass of grey and yellow putrefaction. The hospital itself was a scene of pre-Florence Nightingale Crimean War horror. The doors were smashed and hanging off their hinges. Bandages and some drugs were piled up against a broken window covered in filth. The buzzing sound of flies and the smell of infected human flesh hit you the moment you stepped into the hospital, but there was another smell too, a smell that cut across your teeth with its sharpness, a smell of iron and meat. It took a moment to work out what it was, but then the awfulness of it hit you: it was the smell of blood, some of it old and covering the whole floor a couple of millimetres deep, some of it just recently dried, and some of it fresh from the wounds of the soldiers.

Two men, one with a chest wound and the other with his leg shot or blown to shreds lay on a pair of rickety hospital beds in the ward. The mattresses they lay on were black and shiny as a polished shoe with caked layers of old dried blood. The man with the chest wound looked like he wasn't going to make it. His breathing was shallow and hoarse with pain − a pitiful, frightening, sound this death rattle. His face was convulsed by his suffering, taut and angular like those carved Zairean masks that you can now buy at the flea markets in Johannesburg, and his eyes were deep brown wells of fear, utter hopelessness and agony.

An orderly in a filthy coat stepped outside with a box of dirty, pus-filled bandages and used syringes. He walked perhaps three metres away from the outside door of the ward and threw all that infected medical waste into the mud where I had seen barefoot children walking a few minutes before.

A wave of irrational rage came over me, I wanted to grab him by the lapels of his dirty coat and scream at him: 'What the fuck do you think you are doing? Haven't you heard of the most basic techniques of hygiene?'

But, of course, I said nothing. I'd seen enough of Angola, and of the war to know that I couldn't judge anymore, to know that I couldn't be sure what I would have done in his place, living this reality day in and day out.

We got to the UN house where we were staying just as dark was falling. In what remained of the garden there was a shallow earth-covered bunker and a deep shell hole in the street just outside where a mortar bomb had hit only a few days before. There were two MPLA guards with AK-47s sitting on the balcony. Inside, there were a few beat-up chairs scattered around and, tacked to the wall, the beautiful, silvery skin of a leopard that had been killed in the bush nearby and given to the UN delegation as a gift.

Pierre, a young Frenchman, who had been a paratrooper in France and now worked for the UN distributing emergency food aid, welcomed us and motioned for us to sit down around the makeshift dining-room table. Our dinner was a mixture of NATO-issue ration packs and some food scrounged from somewhere around town: spam, goat meat, rice, dark, tiny brown mushrooms which still were coated with grains of sand. There was no electricity, so we ate by the light of crude lamps made of wicks of cotton wool floating in a saucer of UN-donated cooking oil. As the light outside faded, the flickering glimmer of the lamps cast huge uneasy shadows on the walls around us.

UNITA was all around us in the bush nearby. The most recent assault on the town had been the night before last, but Pierre assured us that there would be fighting tonight — 'there is fighting every night.'

On this side of the war, UNITA was the enemy you never saw. The unseen source of all the fear that filled every conversation in this country, and that woke you, your heart pounding, in the middle of the night, waiting, always, for that moment when they did, finally, come.

But I had been to the other side of the war, years ago, at the start of my career in journalism. It was another lifetime then, another world, where we took off in an SADF Dakota before dawn from Wonderboom airport outside Pretoria, and by the time there was enough light to see properly we were flying low somewhere in southern Angola. The plane skimmed over the bush at treetop level, perhaps 100 metres above ground, flying so low to avoid being picked up by the Russian and East German radar.

We landed somewhere on a bright sandy runway in the remote bush of Cuando Cubango province, somewhere in the middle of the vast south-eastern Angolan wilderness that the Portuguese had called 'The Land at the End of the Earth', and where the fighting had been so bad that many Angolans now called it 'The Land at the End of Life'.

They put us hacks in the back of a large Tata lorry and drove us around in circles in the bush for nearly eight hours to confuse us. Perhaps an hour's drive was all that would have been necessary, and we arrived at sunset at Jamba, the main UNITA base, suffering from extreme thirst and heat exhaustion.

After dinner there was a briefing from a UNITA officer about 'the military situation in Angola'. They crammed us all into a small straw rondavel with a large map of Angola on a tripod in the front of the room. An officer with a swagger stick pointed to places on the map where the enemy had bases. Here was SWAPO, here MPLA, here ANC. UNITA had won victories here and here, and there. It was only a matter of time before UNITA crushed the enemy here and advanced there...

The next day we filmed a UNITA parade. The soldiers marching up and down in the sun on the hot parade ground, the one captured Russian tank emerging from behind the podium and trundling onto the square to a chorus of wild cheering from the UNITA faithful gathered ten-deep around. Then Savimbi himself, striding purposefully up to the podium and speaking for hours in Portuguese, and, for the benefit of the hastily-turned on TV cameras, for a few minutes in

English on his relationship with Pretoria and (tentatively) how reform was needed of the apartheid system.

At last the ceremony was over, and Savimbi had returned to his private bunker. We were only flying back to South Africa the next morning, so we had a few hours in the late afternoon to relax and wander the few hundred metres around Jamba that we were allowed to. A young teenage soldier had been assigned to guard a few of us who wanted to walk around a bit. The boy spoke no English at all, and only a few words of rudimentary Portuguese. He was short but was fit and very muscular. He held his AK-47 proudly across his chest, and indicated with a small brisk movement of either the barrel or the butt where we could and couldn't go. Despite his military bearing, he seemed shy and, underneath it all, wanting to be friendly. But whenever he smiled, he revealed a set of teeth that had been filed into sharp conical points. It seemed to me then to be a ferocious self-mutilation that must have come from a sensitive, young mind exposed too early to the horrors of war, or, perhaps, an ancient tribal custom that was still practised in these remote parts of Africa.

As the sun was setting and the heat of the day had cooled somewhat, our guard led us back towards the parade ground where a group of soldiers had gathered to play soccer. It could have been a scene anywhere on the continent. I still remember, so clearly, the dust being kicked up and hanging in the golden afternoon light as they passed the ball to one another, the shouts of excitement and the low murmurs of disappointment as the game progressed, and the delighted laughter of the spectators.

But that was all a long time ago. Now, tonight, UNITA was in the darkness on the edge of town. And we were sleeping behind MPLA lines. If UNITA did come, tonight, who knew what might happen. I couldn't help thinking of the irony of it all. I had been to Jamba. I had seen that boy-soldier's shy, uneasy smile that, in truth, (and I only found this out years later) had been a tribal custom, but was one that had a brutal origin. In the days of the slave trade one of the ways of determining a slave's potential value was by examining the state of his or her teeth. The people in that region of Angola had started mutilating their teeth generations ago so that the slavers wouldn't take them. After learning that, I always wondered whether that soldier knew the reason why his teeth had been ruined. For myself, I knew that I would never be able to forget his smile.

And I had seen the UNITA soldiers playing soccer in the beautiful fading light of a bush afternoon, and, if I tried, I could still hear them laughing and shouting over the thump of the ball being kicked around.

It had been a short visit and it was, I knew, nothing more than a fleeting contact with their humanity, but as the darkness fell over Luena I knew that that visit had been enough to keep the seductive ghosts of stereotype away. In the broad moral scope of Angola's suffering, there was no question that Savimbi and UNITA were to blame for this new war, but, at the same time, I couldn't see UNITA as just a faceless 'enemy'. For all I knew, that boy-soldier of the past was somewhere in the bush around us, smiling in the darkness.

Within minutes of night falling, the firing began. All over the town, in the distance, and then suddenly nearby and frighteningly loud — in the street right next to us, and then, far away again, muffled by the ruined houses. There was the brittle pop-pop-pop-pop of AK-47 fire and the heavy crash-crash-crash-crash of 50 mm anti-aircraft machine guns, lowered right down, firing horizontally into the bush around us.

Most of it was definitely outgoing, just panicky MPLA troops blazing away at any sound, imagined or otherwise. Occasionally, there was the distant sound of what could have been incoming, but we were lucky that night, we never had the dubious luxury of being sure. And neither did the MPLA, and when we heard what might have been incoming, they opened up and there was the sudden frantic arc of cherry-red tracer cutting across the darkness of the sky, and sometimes a parachute flare lighting up the trees and the ruined houses for a breathstopping long beautiful moment while the gunfire

increased and then died as the bright phosphorus light
burned out and the darkness came back.

The shooting died down for a time, and it was so hot inside
we went to sit in the deep shadows of the balcony. Our guards
stirred uneasily as we came out, conscious of the increased
responsibility. We offered them cigarettes, as a gesture of
friendship. They took them, and smoked them inside their
fists, so that the glow of the tip was completely invisible.

There was the smell of tobacco drifting across the open
space that separated them from us, and it was incredibly
sublime and peaceful, that lull in the shooting. We sat talking
quietly in the darkness for a while. There was a full moon and
the black clearness of night surrounded us, with huge rain
clouds beginning to collect overhead and scudding by like a
herd of silent, grey elephants. The stars between them were
like tiny, glittering birds, and we pointed out the Milky Way,
Cassiopeia and the Southern Cross to one another. Over the
horizon there was a storm breaking loose, and we could see
the flashes of lightning bringing the rains that the parched
land needed so desperately, but which the war would allow to
flow meaninglessly away. The peasants would not be able to
cultivate in the midst of the land mines and the fighting. In
the garden, the silver moonlight shone on the frangipani, and
it was so bright and sharp that the ribs in the broad leaves
stood out like ripples on tiny pools of water.

And then, again, a roar of machine-gun fire tore through
the darkness nearby. Pierre stood up. 'I think we'd better go
inside.'

The next day, when we got back to Luanda, there was a letter
for me at the hotel's reception desk. It was from Leen
Revalier, the head of the Red Cross centre in Viana. 'Chico
wanted me to give this to you,' he had written. I unrolled the
piece of paper. It was a drawing. A child's drawing. Chico's
drawing. Just looking at it, I suddenly found myself having to
choke back tears in the hotel lobby. It was a self-portrait of
Chico. He stood in the middle of the drawing, a crude stick
figure with hair sticking up in little lines, crutches in his
hands and a square stump where his right leg should be.

Around him were abstract figures all drawn with sharp, angular lines, and a strange, disembodied head with what appeared to be blood pouring from the skull. There it was: the explosion, the chaos, the fear, the anger, the pain... it was all there on the paper in front of me. Chico's story.

Alone in my hotel room, I broke down. I found myself crying for Chico, and through him, for the *mutilados*, for the tens of thousands like them, for the starving refugees and the dying soldiers in the hospital in Luena, for the millions of suffering people all over this agonised country. I found myself crying for the pain that calls itself Angola.

Mark and I were splitting up. He was setting off, armed with the Betacam with a group of journalists who were joining a military column that was going to try to get through to Huambo. I was to carry on working with Teresa and shooting with a Hi-8 and get whatever we could. Judith Matloff had been transferred back to Johannesburg for a much-needed rest and Robert Powell from the Lisbon bureau was joining us. There was suddenly a wave of interest from the outside world in Angola. Tom Carver from the BBC had flown up from Jo'burg along with a dozen or more TV, radio and print journalists.

We all had dinner that night together at *Afrodiziak* out on the Ilha. We discussed our plans. The rumour was that the fighting was going badly for the government in Huambo. It was said that the city was on the verge of falling to UNITA. Almost everybody around the table wanted to join Mark and the others on the military column. They had been sent by their editors to try get to Huambo if at all possible — it seemed that suddenly the world cared about Angola.

The next few days passed in a blur of trying to squeeze stories out of Luanda. We did a story on the cholera outbreak in the city, we filmed at the civilian hospital, at the military hospital. We interviewed Margaret Anstee, the head of the UN delegation in Angola. All the while, there was no news from Mark and the column, so we assumed that he was all right. The work we were doing was all solid, worthwhile journalism and our offices in Johannesburg and London seemed pleased with the results. But the real war was outside Luanda, and it was frustrating to be stuck inside the capital when we had come to try and report the reality of what was happening in Angola. I wanted to see Chico, too, to thank him for giving me his painting. But there was never time to go during the day, and it was unthinkable to try and drive outside the city after dark. Still, I found myself often thinking of Chico and his drawing. Somehow, it had changed Angola for me; it was no longer just a story to me. Chico had taught me something, but I couldn't quite express what it was. It was just there, making me see things in a different way.

So we waited, and did what we could, and tried to get on WFP flights to other parts of the country. To go anywhere, to get out of Luanda, to fly up above the sea of rumours that washed around us every day and see what was happening for ourselves.

Luanda's night life continued unabated. Somehow, through all the misery and the choking constraints of the war (the MiGs were booming over the city most of the day, making their bombing runs at Caxito) people managed to construct a life for themselves. They hated the war, and the suffering, but they had decided to enjoy themselves as much as they could. It was perhaps the thing I admired most about the Angolans, their refusal to let their horrific circumstances rule their attitude to life.

One night there was a party at the Belgian ambassador's house up on the Miramar. The Miramar (seaview) was once one of the world's most beautiful suburbs. The sixties style chrome-and-abstract mansions of the last colonial rich still line the steep hill that overlooks Luanda bay, and, at night, (when the electricity is working) the lights of the city gleam up through the darkness and, even without trying, one can recreate the illusion that Luanda is a beautiful exotic metropolis.

I remember standing on the terrazzo balcony talking to Teresa with the indescribably beautiful sinuous black and mulatto Angolan girls dancing to the Brazilian music with their chic male partners behind me, a cold beer in my hand and the false promise of the lights of the city below us. I was slightly drunk, and taken with the emotion of the moment. 'This,' I said, 'is how Angola should be.'

'This,' Teresa replied, 'was how Angola was, but only for whites.'

One night, Robert Powell and I came home from a dinner on the Ilha. There was a fax for him from the Reuters office in Lisbon. According to a report monitored in Lisbon, the government had announced a 'strategic withdrawal' from Huambo.

It was a Friday night, so for the next two days we could get no confirmation from the government. The defence ministry brooded in blank, unmoving silence over the torpor of the city, but, Radio Vorgen, the Voice of the Black Cockerel, UNITA radio was filling the airwaves with the news that Huambo had fallen.

Cubal was the nearest anyone could get to Huambo. At the outbreak of the 'new' war UNITA had captured it but it had been retaken only few weeks before by the government, and was now, with the fall of Huambo, their main base in the central highlands of Angola. There was a WFP flight to Cubal and Robert Powell and I managed to get on it somehow. There was the same reddened dawn at the airport, the same jolting rise into the air on an ageing Antonov, disappearing into the impossibly blue sky and landing with a hard bump and a smoke of burning rubber on the airstrip. The troops on the runway were hard-faced and angry, and kicked and pushed the skinny civilians who tried to grab at the food aid bags. Once or twice one of them raised his AK-47 as if to fire a burst into the air and the civilians retreated, cowering back only a few metres.

We met up with Marco, a freelance Belgian photographer whom we knew slightly from Luanda. He was extremely well-connected and always willing to help. The situation was a little scary because, there was no doubt about it, the war was coming this way. Fast. It was sweeping west over the country from Huambo like a vast, consuming wind. You could see it in the crazy, hard faces of the soldiers and the ragged desperation of the civilians. As we drove into town we could hear the distant thud of mortars echoing somewhere in the bush behind the low hills that surrounded the town. Incoming and outgoing. They were still far, but close enough that the UNITA forward units could probably be at the edges of the town in a day, or less.

Strings of refugees poured into town and across the countryside. They were the first part of the shock wave of humanity fleeing from Huambo. Most of them were not from the city itself but were peasants from the outlying districts carrying their few belongings on their heads or in their hands. A very few had pushcarts piled high with clothes, bags of grain, chickens, a couple of rough-hewn chairs — most had nothing but the filthy clothes they were wearing.

All day the people streamed in behind the front lines into the small, picturesque town of Cubal, its main street lined with whitewashed buildings and spreading flame trees and then beyond, heading for the haven of Benguela still 200 kilometres away, on top of the 200-odd kilometres many of them had already walked. At first, I filmed lots of footage of the lines of refugees slowly treading through the shimmering heat waves on the horizon, but then, in the end I stopped, because there were so many of them they simply became a backdrop to the military activity. The soldiers ignored them, or treated them like dirt, and the refugees, in turn, steered clear of the battle-touched soldiers, keeping their eyes on the ground and pretending not to exist when they passed them.

At the same time, while they feared the MPLA troops, it was clear that they hated UNITA. 'UNITA caught me and beat me,' one man told us. 'Then they made me eat my party card.'

'The journey was not an easy one,' a woman said. 'Many of the injured died on the way, some of them were too weak to climb over mountains and rivers. I saw a woman die on the roadside trying to give birth to her baby. UNITA attacked us on the road and many people died in their ambushes.'

'It's war now,' said another. 'I want to pick up a gun.'

Then there were the rumours. 'There are white men fighting with UNITA. They have radios.'

At the time there was continuing debate about whether some of the old guard of the SADF were supporting UNITA clandestinely. Confirmation on a story like that would have been a real journalistic breakthrough — a 'scoop', if you like. But there never was any confirmation of these stories. When pressed, the people could never say they had seen the whites themselves. It was always someone else who had seen it, or they had heard the story from someone who knew someone who had seen the mercenaries.

Then there was my personal favourite, told to me by some MPLA officers on the front lines: 'When UNITA catches journalists, they pull their eyes out, hack off their ears and cut off their fingers.'

There it is, scribbled in my notebook. I would be lying if I said there wasn't a part of me that didn't believe it. It was like the sewers, and the gunfire in the darkness — the terrors of that you heard spoken of, but hadn't seen, and the horrors of what you had actually seen, but still couldn't believe, started to merge in your brain after a while. The constraints of journalism kept you from believing everything, but, at the same time, what you wrote said hardly anything about what you had really seen and what you really believed.

Somebody offered us a lift to the front defensive lines on the open back of a flat-bed truck. We were helped onto the back by the troops standing there. Before we had got on properly, the driver jammed the vehicle into gear and roared off at high speed with Robert and me trying to clamber up and hang on at the same time. (Marco had somehow disappeared to find his own way to the front.) Finally we managed to get a grip on some wooden poles that were stuck into the side of the steel platform. The driver roared and zigzagged across the countryside and all of us had to hang on, literally with all our strength, to stop ourselves falling off at seventy or eighty kilometres an hour. It was ridiculous, and would have been funny if it hadn't been so dangerous. Some of the soldiers were banging on the cab to indicate to the driver to slow down, but he paid absolutely no attention. He simply clashed the gears, swung the steering wheel and pushed down on the accelerator.

Finally, he pulled up in front of a collection of military tents and a pair of Alouette helicopters parked on the ground nearby. Robert and I jumped off as quickly as possible.

The troops here were both bored and spooked at the same time. They were dug in deep, but living in appalling conditions, and waiting for the battle they knew must come. They, too, could hear the distant mortars, and knew that it was only a matter of time before the shells came screaming down on them. They gathered around us in a huge clump; raining questions at us in Portuguese. I could only understand ten per cent of what was being said, but Robert was handing out cigarettes, speaking to them and jotting furiously in his notebook.

I walked a little bit away and started filming the trenches. Immediately the crowd of soldiers left Robert and swarmed over to where I was pointing the camera. They immediately started hamming it up like the actors in a pantomime. They grabbed up their AK-47s and pointed them forward in ludicrous angles at an imaginary enemy, they rolled their eyes in mock fear, and started prancing along the length of the trenches, lifting their knees and swinging their elbows in exaggerated motions of stalking an enemy; some of them even started going *pshew-pshew-pshew-pshew* and shaking their guns like children playing war games.

They were having a little light relief at my expense, and, I suppose, if you wanted to analyse it, at the expense of the news editors back in London and New York who had suddenly decided that the Angola story 'needed doing'. It was an irony that was laughable, here I was in the middle of some of the most dynamic images of Angola's suffering, and the only pictures I could get were of soldiers behaving like jackasses.

We spent hours walking up and down the defensive positions in the blazing sun. Helicopters rose up behind the hills and cut back and forth across the heat-bleached sky, young recruits jogged along behind the trenches, their NCOs screaming orders at them, armoured cars with machine guns mounted on the top (a couple of them with blackened goat carcasses tied to the side with wire) roared up and down the dirt track roads. There was activity everywhere but, at the same time, nothing seemed to be happening. Everywhere there was the heat, the discomfort, the lines of refugees, and the hidden, invisible strain of the waiting...

At one point, I tried to get some more shots of the refugees pouring in across the front lines. One or two of the teenagers started breakdancing in front of the camera. I moved across the road and set up the tripod. There they were again, grinning into the camera, ruining the shot.

A police corporal standing nearby suddenly went berserk. He picked up a rock half the size of a football and charged at the boys. He made as if he was going to hurl the rock at their heads. They scattered and started running down the road. He was screaming at them as he pulled out his battered Soviet-issue pistol, cocked it, and aimed it in their direction. He stood there for quite a while, holding his pistol and yelling at no one in particular while the refugees melted away off the side of the road.

Finally, he came back to where I was standing. He had a sullen, angry expression on his face. *'Filmar'* he said to me, waving his hand across the empty road.

Late in the afternoon, we met up with Marco again on the runway. There had been a mix-up and all three of us had missed the last WFP flight back to Luanda. Robert and I had walked back to the airport, but we had arrived too late to catch the flight. None of us wanted to stay in Cubal that night, and the only chance of getting a flight out was to hitch a ride on a military chopper for Benguela. Marco knew the local commander slightly so we left him to organise it.

All around us, the drive to recruit soldiers was in full swing. Groups of men and boys were assembled in crooked lines across the tarmac, huge piles of AK-47s, webbing and uniforms in front of them. One by one they were called forward, their names were noted by an orderly in an exercise book, and they were issued a rifle, webbing and a uniform.

A group of about fifty boys, not one of them older than nineteen, stood in a line in front of large orange and blue Soviet transport helicopter. They were schoolboys who had been called up for military service, and had somehow been shortlisted to be flown to Benguela for specialised training. Rural peasant boys from the countryside around Cubal, most of them had hardly been in a motor vehicle, and certainly none of them had ever flown in an aeroplane or a helicopter before. They were pushing and shoving one another in their eagerness to be first. One boy got a split lip from bumping into the boy in front of him when he tried to jump the queue, and the others all laughed at him and sent him right to the back where he sulked and endured the taunts of his mates.

Marco had persuaded the commander to allow the three of us to fly out on the same helicopter, and the group of boys had to wait while we, and a couple of other officers, climbed on and found ourselves seats. Marco insisted on placing himself at the open side door, and the boys chosen to get on the flight, twenty-seven of them, had to push past him as they climbed up into the maw of the chopper with its scratched aluminium fittings and worn Russian writing inside.

We took off into the late afternoon sunlight, the long, curving blades of the chopper picking up speed and then starting to roar and shake the whole machine. We travelled forward a few metres and then pitched forward and lifted into the sky. There was another chopper flying with us. It was armed with rocket launchers and flew in front, providing cover in case of an attack by UNITA. The first few kilometres were the most dangerous because that was how close UNITA was to the town. It would only take a few minutes, perhaps ten at most, before we were out of that extreme danger zone, and nobody said anything during that time. We all sat silently watching the trees sweep past under the wheels of the chopper. We were flying literally at treetop level so that UNITA would have as little warning of our approach as possible, and we could sweep over their heads and disappear over the horizon before they had time to fire their RPGs at us. Marco was perched on the edge of the chopper, his feet on the wheel strut, his hair blown back across his scalp, alternately holding his camera in his lap and putting it to his eye, looking for a shot to materialise.

Slowly, and then suddenly, without anything being said, we began to relax. An unannounced, invisible line had been crossed and we felt safer; UNITA was somewhere behind and Benguela lay in front. The sun was sinking low on the horizon, filling the sky with a glorious pink and marmalade light. The landscape below us was covered with miles and miles of baobab trees stretching as far as the eye could see, their bleached white trunks and stunted fans of branches catching the light and glowing with orange and lavender fire, and the soil they clung to was a rich, garnet red. Once the danger was behind us, the chopper ride became a wild, horizontal tumble through an Africa that I have never seen before or since — a mystical wonderland flowing by beneath us, and the western horizon scarlet and gold in front.

We were all tired from the heat of the day and the ever-present strain of the war, but that chopper ride over that sea of baobabs was, for all of us, a moment of mystic intensity where sadness and fear and joy and exhaustion mixed into one indeterminable emotion — the beating heart of the paradox; the pure, undiluted experience of being alive.

I remember trying to reconcile experiencing the beauty of that moment with the certain knowledge of the fate that awaited so many of these boys. Looking at their eager faces in the golden light that shone through the portholes as we hung in the air above that sublime scenery, I recalled another image, just as powerful: the hospital in Luena with the blood-blackened mattresses, the new blood on the floor, the flies, and the hoarse wheezing breath of the soldier dying slowly in terrible pain.

That night in Benguela, the three of us, Robert, Marco and I sat at a café on the ruined boulevard at the edge of the ocean, listening to the waves and looking at the blackness of the hot night sky above us. We drank beer after beer after beer, until none of us was making any sense. Sometime in the night, hundreds of crabs came up from the beach and scuttled across the road towards the single light of the café. 'UNITA eats these creatures,' another patron sitting at a table nearby said. 'They make sandwiches out of them while they are still alive, smearing the bread first with toothpaste.'

We tried to chase the crabs away, kicking at them, but they only crawled a little way into the shadows and stared up at us through the darkness with their hard, luminescent eyes.

'EM. PEE. EL. AAH. MPLA, MPLA, MPLA!' The chant quickened and spread along the side of the road as we streamed into Caxito. Teresa and Robert and I were on the back of a truck full of MPLA soldiers coming to reinforce their battle-weary comrades. The fortunes of war had swung in the government's favour. Two days ago government forces retook Caxito, driving UNITA back into the bush, and relieving some of the pressure on Luanda. The press had full permission to cover the story. The peasants were all rushing up to the side of the road, cheering and waving as we drove past. The soldiers we were with were heavily armed. Two or three on the truck had been posted as guards and they stood alert behind the cab, holding their rifles at the ready, their eyes scanning the thick green vegetation on either side of us for the remnants of the UNITA forces who were still hiding in the bush.

UNITA had fled hastily, leaving at least one heavy gun behind, its piles of spent shells bearing both Russian and American markings — according to the peace agreements neither of those two countries was supposed to be supplying arms to either side, so the arms dealers now filled the gap with arms from either country to both sides, paid for in diamonds and oil.

There were unexploded mortar shells in the sand all along the road, and abandoned bayonets, machetes, AK-47 magazines (the rifles themselves, along with the bodies, had already been gathered up). But the recent heat of battle was still in the eyes of the troops that passed us in tanks and trucks rushing to and from the now-expanding front. They were all wildly pleased to see us and our cameras, marking their victory, immortalising their moment in history and they waved and chanted as we passed them 'MPLA, MPLA, MPLA...'

The passions and the craziness of war were everywhere. There was still gunfire crashing through the streets when we drove into town, as the government soldiers both celebrated and concentrated on making sure there were no UNITA troops hiding in the abandoned shops and houses. Behind the shattered, bullet-scarred façade of the bank, there was the skeleton of a soldier, UNITA or MPLA, we couldn't tell, we only knew it was a soldier from the rotting combat boot half-buried in the sandy soil.

An LMG opened up nearby, hammering heavy bullets into the houses around us, and Teresa and I hurried back to the openness of the main street where there could be no mistake about who we were.

Further up the street, some MPLA troops had caught a teenage boy they claimed was a UNITA soldier. They had tied his arms behind his back with a loop of fencing wire fastened tight above his elbows, cutting off the flow of blood. Thirty minutes of that and he would lose his arms. They were kicking and pushing him into the cab of a truck to take him to their commander for interrogation. We got in the truck with them and Robert and Teresa pleaded with the soldiers to undo the wire. Finally, they took off the wire and Robert gave the trembling, terrified boy a cigarette.

We arrived at the command post and Robert complained to a senior officer about the treatment of the prisoner. The officer brusquely reprimanded the soldiers, but still the boy was led around the back of the house, a corporal whipping him across the back with a plastic sjambok.

There were hundreds of soldiers swimming and washing themselves in a nearby dam, stripped naked and enjoying the sweet coolness of the water. 'Come on in and join us,' they were shouting at us in Portuguese, and beckoning with their arms. 'It's lovely, come and have a swim!'

A lieutenant stormed out from the shade of a nearby tree. 'GET AWAY FROM HERE,' he screamed at us. 'GET OUT! THIS IS A MILITARY AREA. YOU CANNOT TAKE PHOTOGRAPHS OF SOLDIERS WASHING.'

The bridge across the Dande River had been blown up and the vast concrete pillars lay like crumpled paper in the rushing water. Empty cartridge cases lay as thick as a swarm of bees among the broken folds in the concrete, a mute testimony to the severity of the fighting that had taken place here.

Troops and civilians were being ferried across the river in dugout canoes and a makeshift wooden raft. They were bringing shells across, and the children all lent a hand, standing in a chain handing the shells down to the raft, giggling and laughing with excitement as their skinny arms wrapped themselves around each heavy load of explosive, and passed it on to the next child, just barely managing the weight of it.

Late in the afternoon, when we had finished filming and interviewing people, we started the drive back to Luanda. We were going fairly fast so that Robert could file in time, and all the way along the road, vehicles filled with MPLA troops hooted and cheered as we drove past them. Just a few kilometres down the road, we were waved down by three whites in a battered Peugeot, heading in the direction of Caxito. They were friendly and relaxed, men out on a pleasure-trip. They opened the boot and pulled out ice-cold Sagres beer, and offered it around. We stood there in the middle of the road that, just a few metres away, was lined with mines and blown-up armoured cars. They said they had come from Luanda to do some hunting in the bush around Caxito now that the town was back in government hands. But was the road safe, they wanted to know. They wanted to be in Caxito before nightfall, was the bridge across the river passable?

We told them it wasn't, and suggested that they turn around and go back to Luanda. They seemed disappointed at our kill-joy attitude, especially after they had shared their cold beer with us, and they drove off towards Caxito without once looking back.

Another weekend, my last in Luanda. On Monday Mark is coming back from the column that tried to get to Huambo and we are flying out to Windhoek the next day.

Everything is a rush to get organised, but I manage to get the afternoon free to go out to Viana to visit Chico. Teresa and I stop off at the open-air market to buy crayons and exercise books for Chico, and, for ourselves, we buy a couple of Fantas and a bag of roasted peanuts.

We pull into the hospital grounds in the dead heat of afternoon. It is Sunday, so the Red Cross staff has the day off, and it is just the patients sitting in the shade. And there is Chico, he has seen us almost immediately and he is swinging his way towards us on his crutches as fast as he can. The two of us get out of the car with the notebooks and crayons. Chico is happy to see us and he smiles broadly. I ask Teresa to thank him for the drawing, and he nods, looking down at the ground.

From the prefab sheds in front of us, another little boy emerges. One of the adult patients tells us that he, too, is an orphan who arrived at the centre last week. He is mute, and cannot say a word, but the doctors can find nothing physically wrong with him. They think it is psychological, that he has subconsciously decided he will not speak of the horrors he has seen.

The boy shuffles over to us and Chico. He stands there looking at the crayons and the notebooks; his face is utterly bland and expressionless. Teresa and I are stricken with panic in the way adults are when they know they have hurt a child's feelings. We have no present for this little boy. Then we remember the Fantas and the bag of peanuts. Teresa reaches into the car and brings them out. When she hands them to the boy, he smiles — a glorious, brilliant smile. A smile of pure joy that spreads almost across his whole face. I have never in my life seen a smile more filled with hidden laughter and a longing to reach out. It is almost as if his facial expressions have become more acute in order to make up for his inability to speak.

He can hardly contain his excitement at the presents, and he rushes back across the open quadrangle towards his bed to stash them. When you live so casually in the midst of affluence, as most of us do, it is humbling to see how much joy a simple bag of peanuts and a tin of warm Fanta can bring to a lonely child.

Chico is more contained. He stands around with us while we chat to some of the adult patients and hand out the last of the cigarettes we have brought with us. And then it is time to leave. This time as we drive out Chico does not wave, he just stands and watches us turn out of the gate.

It is only when we are driving back to Luanda, through the garbage and the war-scarred suburbs that I finally realise what it is that Chico, and his friend, have taught me. Between the two of them, they showed me that no matter what human beings have suffered, no matter how their lives have been twisted by the double workings of both fate and cruelty, love is still always possible. It cannot be guaranteed, but, yes, even if it can only be expressed in modest, even small ways, it is always possible.

CHAPTER 6

FLOUR IN THE SAME SACK

The huge mouth of the Zaire River filled the horizon, a brown arc stretching across the periphery of the eye's vision. Heavy white clouds hung low over the wide flowing mass of dirty fresh water spewing out into the ocean, and the air above it was filled with a muggy haze of humidity. In a matter of minutes we flew past the small spit of land that is the republic of Zaire's only link to the sea and were back in Angolan territory, in Cabinda.

Cabinda is one of Africa's half-forgotten corners. A sleepy enclave of Angolan territory just over 7 200 square kilometres in size, it is surrounded by Zaire and the Congo Republic and has a population of about 100 000. It was first settled by the Dutch and the Portuguese took over in 1886.

Today, it is the site of a completely different war on Angolan territory. UNITA is militarily inactive in Cabinda, but for some twenty years FLEC (Front for the Liberation of the Enclave of Cabinda) has been fighting a low-level insurgency to gain independence. After the 1991 peace accords between UNITA and the MPLA, FLEC felt left out and increased its level of activity. The main reason for all the fuss is that Cabinda has oil. The province produces over 300 000 barrels of crude oil a day, amounting to some three per cent of U.S. oil imports. (It was one of the Cold War ironies that at the same time that Ronald Reagan's government was voting to send Stinger missiles to UNITA, the communist MPLA's war effort was supported very largely by oil sales to America through Cabinda Gulf, a subsidiary of Gulf Oil.)

Now that Walvis Bay has been returned to Namibia, and Eritrea has finally gained its independence from Ethiopia, the question of independence for Cabinda, like the Moroccan occupation of Western Sahara, is one of the last unresolved sovereignty issues in post-colonial Africa.

In some ways, the Cabindan issue, at the moment, is little more than a postscript to the situation in Angola itself, but the issues arising out of FLEC's claims for independence are potentially far more wide-reaching than this, for Angola's claim to retain control of the territory is based on the OAU's founding declaration on the sanctity of colonial boundaries in 1963. Challenging this claim successfully could call into question the entire principle on which every modern African nation state is founded. Independence for Cabinda could possibly lead to renewed calls for the independence of Katanga or of KwaZulu/Natal. Even if that didn't happen, the loss of control over the oil revenue would certainly have serious implications for Angola's balance of payments.

Cabinda is one of the last colonies in Africa. What makes it particularly interesting is that it is an African colony once ruled by Europeans and now ruled by Africans from another country and another society who have simply taken over from where the European occupiers left off.

The mouth of the river disappeared behind us, and the pilot banked and started descending towards Cabinda city; beneath us a patchwork of green fields was spread out just behind the white sands of the coast line: cassava, manioc, corn with mango and paw-paw trees interspersed between the fields. And then the town of Cabinda itself appeared with the corrugated roofs of the buildings shimmering in the muggy heat like patches of water.

The plane did a turn over the ocean and then rushed in at the black tarmac landing strip of the airport. Even though it was only nine in the morning, Robert Powell and I climbed out of the plane into sauna-like heat and humidity. There was the salt air and another aroma I wasn't familiar with. It took me a moment or two to work it out: it was the musty, moist vegetable smell of the jungle. Tall, lacy coconut palms swayed in the warm breeze. The women waiting at the edge of the runway for the next plane were dressed in the vividly coloured cotton dresses and headwraps of Zaire. The men, like men were dressed in Bart Simpson and Rambo T-shirts, polyester slacks and imitation Ray-Bans.

At the edge of the runway, there was a group of gleaming helicopters waiting, each with an American pilot sitting patiently at the controls.

I took the camera over to where the helicopters stood, and started filming.

'Hey, guy,' one of them called across to me. 'I'm not too sure the authorities here would want you to be doing that.'

'I think it'll be all right,' I told him. 'I'm not shooting anything military.'

He laughed. 'Yeah, that would definitely get you in some kind of deep shit.'

After I had taken a couple of shots, I went over to talk to the pilot. He was the archetypal middle-aged American pilot who flew overseas: Ray-Ban Aviators, two-day old stubble on his chin, a lean, tough physique and an air of wisecracking reserve that hinted at earlier glory years of secret runs for Air America on moonless nights above the jungle on the Cambodian border, and landing in a Huey on the hard sand just above the breakers at China Beach to drop off an ice-cold six pack for some Marine buddies catching a tan on a three-day R 'n R stint.

What, I wanted to know, was he doing here, in Cabinda?

'We're waiting for expatriate personnel that arrived on the flight with you to clear customs, and then we ferry them out to the company compound at Malongo.'

Did all the expats fly to Malongo now instead of taking the road?

'Yeah, there's too many ambushes along that road now. Just the other day, a UN guy got kidnapped. If you ask me, FLEC's got the government on the run here.'

I hadn't specifically asked about FLEC. In fact, I had assumed that chopper rides for expat personnel were simply an expected extravagance for an oil company, but it was interesting, and surprising, to know how seriously the FLEC insurgency was being taken by Cabinda Gulf, at least.

There were no taxis at the airport. But somehow Robert managed to arrange for someone to take us into town in a battered Datsun 120Y sedan. The narrow strip of tarmac that led through the jungle into town was surrounded on either side by small wooden and corrugated iron houses amidst the dense green vegetation and groves of gigantic bamboo that towered above the road like a storybook version of Africa.

Our first stop was at the Hotel Maiombe, named after the characteristic forests in the area. Two smartly-dressed Angolan army ninjas (complete with mirror sunglasses) stood at attention outside the door. Inside the air-conditioned foyer there were a few senior military officers lounging around on the leather-covered chairs.

At reception, while we were checking in, the manager suddenly appeared behind the counter. He was a white Portuguese who had served in the Portuguese army as a paratrooper some years before.

We had to wait while our credit cards were checked.

'I'm sorry I cannot offer you a seat,' the manager said, 'but we have important guests here at the moment. There are some generals up from Luanda.'

'Are they discussing the military situation?' Robert asked, his journalist's instinct aroused.

'I think so.'

The manager smiled. 'So, you are journalists, then?'

'Yes.'

'How long are you here for?'

'We leave again early tomorrow afternoon.'

'I hope you enjoy your stay here in Cabinda.'

'I'm sure we will,' Robert replied.

The manager bowed his head slightly in the gracious way that the Portuguese seem to have picked up from their 500-year contact with the East.

'We will do everything in our power to make sure you do.'

We took a taxi back to the centre of town to the local office of the Ministry of Information which was an old Portuguese colonial building. Unlike in other parts of Angola, it was in good repair. The Portuguese had simply walked out one day, and the MPLA authorities had moved in. The wooden sash windows with the grey institutional paint just peeling off in little flakes were open to let the soupy breeze in and the garden outside was bright with flowers. The occasional high, fluted song of birds came drifting in through the open window.

We were shown into the director's office. He was very friendly and wanted to know how things were in Luanda. Better in some ways and worse in others, we told him. That, he said, was always the way things were in Luanda. It was the war that was responsible. Yes, it was the war that was to blame, we agreed.

He nodded his head. The war was at the root of all Angola's problems.

Two young men, Raimundo and Wilson, arrived at the director's door. He called them in, and introduced us. Wilson was to be our driver; and, in addition, a car would be provided by the Ministry of Information. Raimundo was to be our guide in Cabinda. We could go anywhere we wanted, within the city limits. The road to Malongo, in particular, was off-limits. Recently, there had been a number of guerrilla attacks and, just the other week, a member of the UN had been kidnapped along that road. No, the road to Malongo was just too dangerous.

Raimundo was an excellent guide. As journalists, particularly TV journalists, one gets so used to being forcibly accompanied by government minders who try to bully and cajole you into filming what they want you to film, and grumble loudly or adopt a mule-like stubbornness when you try to do anything else. Raimundo was not like that at all. Of course, we could not film military installations, and soldiers, but anything else was perfectly acceptable. He didn't mind me filming through the windscreen down the main street of town. He didn't mind me filming the graffiti on the wall next to the open-air cafe that read in clear, bold letters 'VIVA FLEC', and was such an open display of support for the insurgents. Nor did he mind the shot of the children playing under another huge 'VIVA FLEC' daubed on the wall at the entrance of an apartment block.

In fact, he directed Wilson to drive to one or two more places where there was FLEC graffiti painted on the walls for me to film. Wilson didn't say much, and, as the morning wore on, the expression on his face got more introverted until finally, there was no doubt about it, it was an angry, sullen expression.

'Is there a problem?' I asked Raimundo, in English, about Wilson. He shrugged his shoulders, and waved his hand dismissively.

Cabinda city is a small town, and, by mid-morning, we had finished filming all the FLEC graffiti that we could find. Raimundo suggested that we might like to stop back at the hotel for a drink, and perhaps an early lunch.

It was, we thought, considering the extreme heat and humidity, an excellent idea. When we pulled up in front of the hotel, the ninjas were still standing guard outside, but there was also a gleaming, air-conditioned 4x4 parked in front of us.

Raimundo got out and opened the door for us. 'We'll see you later, at two o'clock,' he said.

'But don't you want to join us for lunch?'

'We are busy. We'll see you later.' He climbed into the passenger seat of the car and the two of them drove off.

From inside the bar, we could still see the officers lounging on the chairs in the foyer. They looked bored; the meeting upstairs had obviously been going on for a long time.

We ordered espresso and croissants. 'Baked here in the hotel,' the bartender told us. The coffee was good, strong and sweet, but the croissants were just extraordinary. They were just out of the oven, and were still warm. They were made of the lightest flour and were dusted with a faint coating of sieved sugar that melted on your tongue.

The bartender was pleased that we enjoyed them so much. He brought another two without our even asking, and then leant against the counter to talk to us. 'You are journalists? How do you find Cabinda?'

'The food is excellent.'

'And the people?'

'Very friendly.'

We chatted for a while about inconsequential things, until, slowly, inexorably, the conversation turned to politics.

'Ah, yes, FLEC.' He took our cups and turned back to the bar to fill them with fresh espresso. 'Yes,' he said, putting the hot demitasses back on the polished wooden bar. 'Many people in Cabinda support FLEC.'

We drank our coffee in silence for a while. Outside in the foyer there was the 'ding' of the bell of the lift for the first time since we had come in and the rushing sound of the lift arriving at the ground floor and the doors opening. The officers lounging in the foyer jumped to their feet, and four senior MPLA officers with large numbers of gold insignia on the epaulettes of their otherwise simple combat uniforms, strode meaningfully out across the polished floor.

The manager was there to greet them. Smiling graciously, he shook hands with each one of them. The officers seemed to be in a hurry, but they responded to the manager with loud, cheery greetings, and shook hands in return. He saw them to the door and then slipped ahead to open it for them and usher them politely out into the brutal midday heat.

He came back across the foyer and into the bar where we were sitting.

'There is someone here who would like to see you,' he said. 'Would you please go upstairs to the conference room. They will meet you there in a few minutes.'

The conference room was on the top floor overlooking the city. The whole town of Cabinda stretched out in front of us: red tiled roofs spotted with lichen and houses that had aged gracefully in the wind and humid sea air — here and there the paint peeling off the walls, or a rusty gate hanging off its hinges, nestled in amongst tall, swaying palm trees. Behind the town, the bay was a sweeping pale blue curve with a pair of tugs cutting across the calm water leading a ship into dock. In the far distance, almost hidden in the haze, were the brown plumes of smoke and the tiny flares of orange flame of the oil wells at Malongo, and between us and them, the lush green carpet of the jungle.

The interview with FLEC was going well. 'The people of Cabinda have never intended to integrate with rest of Angola. We want independence. This is another country and the world must accept our reality.'

And what about your relationship with UNITA?

He snorted: 'For us Cabindans both UNITA and the MPLA are flour in the same sack.'

The manager was waiting at reception for us when we went downstairs again. 'Was your meeting useful?' he wanted to know.

'Very,' we told him.

He nodded, and went back in to his office.

It was after lunch. Wilson was at the wheel; Raimundo in the back seat.

'Would you like to see where FLEC attacked the radio station?' Raimundo asked.

'Very much.'

Raimundo leaned forward and said something to Wilson. Wilson slammed the car into gear, grating the metal teeth inside the gearbox terribly, and we roared off down the road.

The attack on the radio station had not been a great military endeavour. There were four bullet scars on the brickwork outside the front of the station and two bullet holes in a pair of windows at the back.

'There was also a mortar bomb,' Raimundo told us. We walked thirty metres, accompanied by the two soldiers who were guarding the station, into the bush where a shallow depression in soft sand marked the point where the mortar bomb had fallen.

'FLEC is not very accurate,' I joked with the soldiers, and Raimundo. They all laughed, and shrugged their shoulders. It was clear that everybody preferred things to be that way.

Late in the afternoon, we managed to persuade the local governor, Augusto Tomas, to give us an interview. 'Cabinda is a special problem that needs special treatment. It is an internal Angolan problem and it is up to Angolans to sit around the table and solve it. Perhaps some sort of autonomy statute can be negotiated...'

After the formal interview was over we had a pleasant chat with Tomas, talking of the war, and a South African company which had recently started doing business in Cabinda, and had sponsored part of the building of a school for Cabindan children. We commented that he seemed less hardline towards FLEC than the official policy emanating from Luanda. He smiled broadly and sat back in his chair. 'Well, I can understand the roots of the problem. After all, I am Cabindan myself.'

Robert and I were the only guests for dinner in the hotel that night. We sat alone in the empty, cavernous dining room of the hotel at a table covered with a formal starched white table cloth and neat rows of silver-plated cutlery. The array of knives and forks and spoons were old and slightly yellowing from being polished almost every day for twenty years. We were surrounded by a forest of starched white tables gleaming with the same silver cutlery. All the other tables stood empty, waiting for diners who would never come. I wondered how the management could afford to keep the hotel running.

In the front of the room there was a huge buffet of soup and meats and salads and fruit. The food on display looked somewhat old and withered, so we ordered *à la carte* instead: a bottle of crisp cold *vinho verde* and a large dish of a superb African fish stew spiced with chilli, garlic and cilantro.

The rain started to pour outside as we ate, huge translucent sheets of water that filled the darkness with noise. The waiters, dressed in formal black slacks and white, waist-length coats, walked over and closed all the windows against the downpour. Then they retreated to the side of the dining room, waiting patiently for more diners, keeping a perfect, inscrutable demeanour, as if there were thirty or forty customers filling the room and they were attending to each one's needs with service of an impeccable standard.

We ordered another bottle of *vinho verde*. The waiter's steps echoed on the dark polished parquet floor as he brought the chilled bottle over to us, weaving his way delicately through the rows of empty tables as if there were a host of invisible diners all around them and he needed to avoid them in his journey to their table.

The rain had stopped, as suddenly as it had begun, and in the quiet that followed it, we could hear the whispered echoes of the kitchen staff behind the swinging doors; and outside huge termites, brought out by the rain, banged relentlessly against the dining-room windows. Their long silvery wings rustled like leaves against the glass until they dropped squirming onto the concrete of the balcony below.

Slightly drunk, Robert and I discussed the meaning of the day's understated events. It was difficult to get a good grip on this story, working out who supported who was a bit like a farcical game of Cluedo. It went something like this: obviously, the manager of the hotel had extensive contact with both sides, and, almost certainly, his own agenda. Further than that, his involvement was unclear. Also, almost every ordinary person we had spoken to, from the barman on, had hinted that they supported FLEC.

Raimundo, of course, was a prime suspect. If he was a FLEC supporter it would explain so much: why he suddenly suggested that we return to the hotel for 'an early lunch' when FLEC just happened to be there, why he willingly took us to every place where FLEC influence could be filmed, completely out of character with every government press minder both Robert and I had dealt with anywhere in the world, and it would explain the mysterious tension between him and Wilson. Wilson was not a FLEC supporter, but it seemed that its influence in the ministry of information was so great that while he grumbled he didn't dare actively refuse to cooperate with Raimundo.

The pieces were starting to fall together nicely, and the picture was clear: FLEC clearly had more support than anyone outside Cabinda supposed — a lot more. The government's tenuous influence seemed to extend only as far as the boundaries of Cabinda city itself, and hardly even that. FLEC was still underground, but only just. Who knew how far their tendrils of influence really stretched. Into the heart of the jungle? Certainly. Into the oil company compound at Malongo? It made sense. Into the local MPLA administration? Absolutely. The only question was: how deep? And what about the governor himself?

Our waiter came over and poured the last of the wine, sharing it equally between our two glasses. We didn't want any more. He put the bottle upside down in the ice-bucket, and then retreated formally, politely and stood waiting for us to finish. His manner was proud and unbending, refusing to admit to the even tiniest flicker of irony or absurdity as he watched the two of us sitting alone, each with our credit cards in our wallets and eating a meal that cost many times the monthly earnings of the average Cabindan, dwarfed by the loneliness and the grandeur of that vast dining room.

He was simply doing things the way he knew they ought to be done — the way they always had been done.

CHAPTER 7

MOZAMBIQUE
PART IV – SQUEAKY SHOES
AND THE MAHARISHI

29

It is cool and restful inside the glistening marble corridors of the Polana Hotel. The polished shoes of all the staff – from porters to the managers – squeak officiously, and somewhat irritatingly, as they walk across the lobby attending to the wishes of yet another guest.

The marble flooring extends beyond the lobby, and the shiny wooden reception desk, into the atrium which is large and cool and filled with potted palms and delicate chinoiserie porcelain vases and ornate cocktail tables surrounded by deep, comfortable couches. Beyond the atrium is the balcony. Wrought-iron tables stand on its tiled floor and the ornate, white-washed parapet is topped with pots of purple bougainvillaea and ivory frangipani. The tables are filled with refined men and women of all races drinking espresso or Perrier water, and picking at the delicious salads that the chef here prepares. They are almost all wearing one or other model of expensive sunglasses and elegant suits and, in the case of the women, simple but exquisitely cut dresses by designers like Issey Miyake or Chanel that show off their firm, well-fed curves. They are all talking animatedly about the administration of aid money or business opportunities in an impressive variety of international languages: Portuguese, French, Italian, English, Japanese, Afrikaans.

Just underneath the balcony is the large geometrically shaped swimming .pool. The water is cool and chemically

Californian-blue, glittering like an opal beneath the shade of the tall coconut palms that sweep up from the smooth green lawn. Beyond the pool is the calm surface of Maputo bay. The magnificent view leads the eye forever eastwards toward Madagascar and, finally, if one want to imagine it, all the way to India.

It is 1993 and the Polana Hotel has been recently refurbished. The official reopening was a grand affair and a number of African leaders, including President de Klerk of South Africa, were invited by the Mozambican government to attend the function.

More importantly, a peace accord has, at last, been signed in Mozambique, and both Frelimo and Renamo have committed themselves to taking part in elections some time in the near future. There are still all sorts of problems with implementing the specifics, and Afonso Dhlakama has not yet come to take up residence in Maputo. Still the prognosis on all sides is mostly optimistic. As the UN Special Representative for Mozambique, Aldo Ajello has been saying for weeks now: 'I am confident the peace process is irreversible. The Mozambicans are tired of war. They want peace.'

30

Myself and cameraman Rob Celliers and TV Tokyo correspondent Yoshi Kamasu are in Maputo to cover the peace settlement and the arrival of fifty-two peacekeeping troops from Japan. It is a historic moment for both countries. For Mozambique, it is a further strengthening of the peace process; for Japan it is only the second time their troops have set foot off Japanese soil since World War II, and their deployment here caused no small controversy back home in Japan.

It is also a personal contrast for Rob. Last time he was at the Polana in the late 1980s it was in a state of total disrepair. There was nothing to eat in the once stately dining room except hard, stale bread and overcooked meat of indeterminable origins, the rooms were in a shocking condition with cockroaches scurrying up the walls and no water to flush the toilet (that had its worn wooden seat held together with a few twists of coat-hanger wire).

On the first landing of the staircase in the old ramshackle Polana there used to hang a beaten copper relief in the shape of the continent of Africa. According to Rob, it was quite a good likeness, but there was one noteworthy feature that caught the viewer's attention immediately — as it was intended to do — and drew one's gaze away from the rest of the continent: somewhere between the 24th and the 28th parallel, the copper map ended abruptly, as if the land south of that had been cut off with a giant knife and taken away. It was not strictly geographically accurate (Maputo itself falls within that latitude) but it was symbolically precise — South Africa, then under apartheid, simply did not exist for the rest of Africa, and, for South Africa, the reverse was equally true.

Today, after you have ordered your Castle beer and your KWV wine, you can dial Jo'burg direct from your hotel room, and the hotel is jampacked with South African tourists on a weekend excursion to watch the South African provincial rugby finals on a Johannesburg pay-TV station beamed straight into the Polana.

31

David is to be our driver for the week or so that we are in Mozambique to cover the arrival and deployment of the Japanese peace-keepers.

He is one of the new breed of entrepreneurs that have sprung up in Maputo recently. He is smartly-dressed in slacks and a silk shirt. On his feet he is wearing expensive patent leather brogues that are polished to a mirror-like gleam, and as he walks across the marble floor of the lobby they squeak in the same conspicuous tone that emanates from the shoes of the hotel staff.

He sits down on the couch opposite us, and he and Yoshi start negotiating a price. Yoshi wants a cut-rate deal. David expresses the opinion that, under the circumstances with all the journalists and foreign aid personnel in town, this would not be possible. Yoshi points out that David is getting a week's guaranteed fare — a lump sum, in cash, and in US dollars. The haggling goes on a little while longer, and soon a price is agreed on.

David's first assignment is to take us to the UN head-quarters where we can get accredited. Of course he knows where it is, almost all his clients, sooner or later, want to go there. The three of us follow David through the — squeak, squeak — marble lobby, and out into the parking lot where his taxi is waiting for us.

He opens the doors, and the boot for our equipment. We spend some time packing the lights and tripod and miscellaneous bits and pieces into the car. When we are finished, David closes and carefully locks the boot. We climb in and close the doors. David goes around to the driver's door. In a smooth, barely noticeable sequence of movements, he slips the brogues off his feet and puts on a pair of Chinese peasant slippers. He reaches in and puts his shoes carefully on a piece of paper specially placed underneath his seat. I am sitting in the front passenger seat and, as David cautiously backs out of his parking place, I can't help noticing that the toes of his shoes are sticking out from under the seat, their polished surfaces just catching the gleam of the hot midday sun.

32

The Mozambique story is not what it used to be. The 'if-it-bleeds-it-leads' school of journalists would no longer find anything newsworthy here. All day we go from press conference to press conference, with, perhaps, an interview here or there thrown in to lighten the day.

David turns out to be a very bad driver, but, at the same time, he is such a gentle, nervous man that none of us has the heart to tell him. At one point, late in the afternoon, Yoshi leaves Rob and me in the car (safely parked) with David while he goes into a building to speak briefly to some Japanese military official.

'Are you at peace with yourself?' David turns in the driver's seat to face us while we are waiting for Yoshi.

Our replies are mumbled, and self-conscious. 'It is important to be at peace,' David tells us, pushing ever so slightly. 'Have you heard of T.M. and the Maharishi Mahesh Yogi?'

'We-ellll, yes,' Rob replies.

David's face takes on an even greater earnestness than it normally possesses.'The Maharishi is very popular here in Mozambique,' he says. 'T.M. is the most important way of thinking about the human mind. Do you know that here even the president and many of his cabinet members practice T.M.?' He hesitates, as if unsure how we will take his next statement. In the end, he decides to speak out anyway: 'You know,' he says, 'it is the teachings of the Maharishi that have finally brought us peace in Mozambique.'

Rob and I say nothing. This is a totally unexpected revelation. We have both covered the war in Mozambique for a number of years, and in all its tragedy and strangeness, we have never before heard talk of T.M. It seems such an odd import to Mozambique, this esoteric philosophy that, in the rest of the world, is gathering dust in the bottom drawer of the faded pyschedelic wardrobe of the 1960s.

33

We fly to Beira for a day with Yoshi. Our taxi driver here turns out to be the exact opposite of David — a cowboy driver prone to fits of apoplectic rage when anything gets in his way. His vehicle is a huge ancient black Mercedes with white smoke that pours from the exhaust every time he changes gear.

The city is still dilapidated and run down, but it is better than it was a few years ago in some respects. There are flowers planted in neat beds around the airport building, the police at the airport are no longer surly and obviously looking for bribes, and, as we drive into town, the atmosphere is more relaxed — there are no military vehicles rushing at high speed, more shops are open and, here and there, informal trading is even taking place on the streets. But the Hotel Dom Carlos is still in a shocking state, and the old lighthouse is still nothing more than a picturesque silhouette against the wide blue sky and the green sea with the dugout canoes surfing in on the white-capped breakers.

34

The road from Beira to the interior — the main route from the capital of Zimbabwe, Harare, to the sea — was, only months before, like the Tete road, a poorly-protected corridor through which convoys of trucks and cars would crawl in a long, frightening ride, always vulnerable to Renamo attacks.

We take a drive twenty or so kilometres down the road — pumping smoke and Portuguese obscenities all the way — long past what was once the safety zone. We pass the Frelimo army barracks where the young soldiers are lounging around in the shade of trees, and on the balcony of the main command building; a few rusty APCs are lying out back, and they already have long elephant grass growing up through the suspension.

The corridor now is patrolled by equally young Italian troops in white-painted UN APCs and open flatbed jeeps that, if an attack did come, would be utterly useless. But the Italian boys are lucky. There has not been a single violation of the cease-fire agreement, and the peace process is now so far advanced that it is unlikely that they will have to engage in any military actions.

The Italian troops wave cheerily as we drive past, and we are given a militarily correct, but very friendly, reception at their camp. The young soldiers seem to be enjoying their tour of duty. The food is good, the sun is warm, and the setting is exotic. 'I like it here,' a paratrooper tells us. 'I never imagined I would come to Africa one day. It is so beautiful.'

35

Back in Maputo the peacekeepers finally arrive. We get shots of the vast Ilutyin transport planes landing at Maputo airport and unloading the mountains of equipment that the Japanese troops will need. We film at the airport until late in the afternoon, and then we go back to the hotel for a couple of drinks in the crowded bar. Like the balcony at lunchtime a few days before, it is packed with people talking business deals.

We get chatting to a group of South Africans and Mozambicans who are putting land deals together. 'Not long ago,' one of the Mozambicans says, 'you could buy a house in Maputo for $2000. But it's no use looking for investment property here anymore. Maputo and Inhaca have already all been snapped up.'

He pauses, and takes a long sip of his Margarita — the Polana Hotel speciality, with coarse salt around the rim of the glass and served on a plate with a tiny live cactus. 'But,' he says, 'if you're interested, I'm putting together a great scheme for investing in beachfront property up in Vilanculos...'

36

The morning before we are to leave, David arrives at the hotel with a pile of T.M. books for Rob and me. He has gone to great trouble to find English, not Portuguese, versions of the pamphlets for us.

'These are for you, my present,' he says as hands them over carefully to us. The two of us flip through them. David watches us impatiently as we page through these precious documents that he has found, these passports to paradise that he wants to share with us. They contain the usual promises of all religious tracts: inner peace, spiritual fulfilment, transcendence of this material world filled with the miseries of birth, old age, disease and death...

After a while, I look up from the page straight into David's face. He is watching Rob and me very intently. His expression is lined with seriousness and anxiety, but his eyes are filled with hope.

CHAPTER 8

THE VALLEYS OF SILENCE

JOHANNESBURG

Basil, from the airport shuttle service company, was helping us to pack. 'I see a lot of wasted space,' he said, and proceeded to repack our medical trunk. He did a good job, rearranging the vast and chaotic array of painkillers, mosquito repellent, bandages and so on that we bought from a chemist in Rosebank. We had four metal trunks full of television equipment, tools, camping gear, sleeping bags, medicines, cooking utensils, rain gear, maps of central and east Africa — the list we drew up at a planning meeting for the trip was at least sixty-nine items long, and there was more besides.

Three of us: Fergal Keane, the correspondent, Glenn Middleton, the cameraman and myself, the sound man, had been asked to work on a documentary on Rwanda for the BBC's Panorama programme. We were flying from the Johannesburg bureau of the BBC to Nairobi where we would meet the director, David Harrison and the producer Rizu Hamid. We had four days to draw up the lists and get what we needed. I phoned Des Wright at the Reuters bureau in Nairobi to get some advice. He had been into Rwanda almost from the moment the massacres began, and had just come out. 'There's nothing left in Rwanda,' he told me. 'You have to take everything with you. Food, cooking pots, water, a generator...' The list got longer and longer as we talked.

Glenn and I rushed from camping shop to camping shop in Johannesburg looking for odd things like waterproof hiking boots (somehow we were told that we were going to be in Rwanda during the rainy season), water purification tablets and energy bars.

Our minds were a confused mass of swirling thoughts, fears and the terrible images that we had seen on TV and in the newspapers. All of us had seen war and killing many times before in Africa, and elsewhere, but we had seen nothing like the myriad heaps of bodies floating down the rivers that flickered on our television screens, we had seen nothing like the endless streams of refugees fleeing the war, nothing like the photographs of the children with their limbs hacked off.

All this slaughter had been taking place while we had been covering the exuberance of South Africa's first democratic election. Rwanda and South Africa lay at the opposite poles of Africa's experience: despair and hope — and the rest of the continent lay somewhere in between.

And, at the same time, like everybody else in the world outside Rwanda, we knew so little about what had happened there, and even less about why it had happened. We were reading whatever we could find to try and catch up, but it was not enough. At that time, we hardly even knew the reasons for the conflict between Hutus and Tutsis. Rwanda was on the news every day, but the reports we saw made little sense to us. There was so much that remained unsaid. The horror of Rwanda was so deep and so fundamental, and yet to confront it in a way that people could understand was difficult.

The genocide in Rwanda illustrated precisely the dilemma of the modern media. The physical evidence of the happenings in the country were, thanks to satellite technology, immediately accessible to the whole world, but, at the same time, how, with limited time on the airwaves, did you so suddenly introduce people to a country they probably had never even heard of before, and then make it clear to them how and why 500 000 people had been killed there in the space of three weeks? How do you cram tiny Rwanda in between the ad breaks? And then there was the difficulty of conveying the sheer enormity of the mass killings. How could you expect people to stomach witnessing genocide over their evening dinner?

You didn't. You couldn't — or, at least, not adequately. The two and a half minute television news clips, the 500-word, (or less), newspaper and magazine stories, the shocking photographs — all they created was a blur of horror that blended with the clichés about tribal war and the 'heart of darkness'. We knew that there had to be much more than this that lay behind such a monstrous human tragedy. The difficulty was in making it comprehensible to the outside world. Our brief was deceptively simple: go to Rwanda and try to make some sense of it all.

Basil was adamant. 'I'm telling you, these won't stop a bullet from a AK or a R1,' he said as he loaded our flak jackets into the minibus that was to take us to the airport.

'They'll be fine,' I replied, a bit shortly. I was nervous and I hate packing flak jackets for a story. The act of packing them is admitting that you are probably going to be putting your life on the line. The flak jackets sitting in the back of the car are tangible evidence of the danger you are going to be confronted with, and, even though these were the best in the world — they had been specially designed to stop high-velocity bullets — I knew they were no real guarantee you would be safe wearing them. Basil's statement was by no means incorrect. He had spent some time as a soldier with 32 Battalion in the Angolan war, which meant that he almost certainly had seen some combat and all the time that we were packing the car, he was giving me a dozen tips on how to survive in a war zone. I ended up in the front seat next to him for the drive out to the airport. For a while, we sat in silence thinking about the journey that lay ahead of us until Basil could bear it no longer.

'Okay,' he conceded as we drove onto the motorway, 'maybe those flak jackets will protect you, but do you know what to do if someone gets bitten by a snake?'

NAIROBI

A new, and distant pulse throbs beneath the usual hustle and bustle of Nairobi's impossibly chaotic streets — it is the faint, outermost ripples of the spiral of madness that has Rwanda at its centre. On the balcony of the Norfolk Hotel, one begins the slow immersion into the state of mind that humankind has called Rwanda. Sitting at groups around tables on the balcony are journalists who have just come out of the country. They are full of tips and hints about what to do and what not to do. Many of them are stills photographers and have taken the greatest risks to get pictures, and yet they are strangely inarticulate, unable to express in words what they have seen and the danger they have felt. Their stories are inside the little film cans marked 'Fuji' and 'Kodak' — and only one or two images will eventually emerge of what they have seen. The rest, hundreds of them, will sit in portfolios in Johannesburg, London, New York and Tokyo gathering dust.

The information they have is invaluable, but it comes in little fragments, in no particular order. You have to concentrate to try and make sense of it, to try and piece it together:

'Whatever you do, don't wear anything military — one guy was wearing a waterbottle with a camouflage pattern on his belt. At one of the roadblocks, the militia hauled him out of the Land Rover, and started screaming "enemy", "enemy" at him.'

'The RPF — the Rwandan Patriotic Front — are cool — as long as you're not French or Belgian. It's the government side that's the problem — especially the militia roadblocks. They stand around with clubs and spears and pangas, fucked on drugs, beer, whatever...'

'I saw some kids walking along the side of the road, dragging clubs in the dust. They were too heavy for them to even lift.'

'You've got to get papers for the government side. You must get a *laissez passer* from the Rwandan ambassador here or, even better, in Burundi, and then, first thing when you are inside the country, you must go to the local prefect of the area and get a letter from him. Without those documents, you're fucked. You won't get anywhere.'

'There's this one place — I can't remember its name, but you'll find it, it's on the main road from Burundi. There's a whole group of Tutsis there behind barbed wire. The army's protecting them, but at night the *interahamwe* come and whack them. They take out about ten a night. There's nothing the army can do. They're also scared of the *interahamwe*.'

The *interahamwe* is the Hutu militia. The name means 'those who stand together'. The *interahamwe* was formed by the Habyarimana government allegedly as a response to the RPF invasion in 1990. They are barely-trained thugs armed with crude clubs and machetes who, together with the Presidential Guard, are alleged to have been behind most of the massacres.

'You must take two vehicles. If you only take one, and it breaks down, you're on your own. You walk, and I wouldn't want to be walking through Rwanda. ITN broke down last week, they had to leave one of their vehicles behind. $11 000 worth.'

'One guy was in there, and he saw them killing a Tutsi. He tried to take some pictures and they told him if he didn't fuck off they would kill all the Tutsis there in front of him. He left, but they almost certainly killed them anyway.'

Snippets — a confusing montage of images and advice, how much is accurate, and how much is exaggerated I will only know when I encounter Rwanda for myself. The process has, however, begun. Already from the stories, the fear has started to seep into my consciousness. The horror remains remote though, filtered through a haze of unreality.

It is difficult to get decent maps of Rwanda. David has brought from London an old Belgian map that still has Rwanda and Burundi marked with the old colonial name Rwanda-Urundi. It was the best he could find there. In Johannesburg, I could find nothing except a general map book of central and southern Africa. Two or three main highways were marked in red on the coin-sized section of paper called Rwanda. 'There's tiny little country roads everywhere,' Joao Da Silva, a photographer from Johannes-burg, tells us. 'On the RPF side you'll have a guide, but on the government side, you'll just have to work things out for yourself.'

At dinner that night, we decided that four of us: David, Fergal, Glen and myself would go to Uganda and make contact with the rebel Rwandan Patriotic Front (RPF) and travel with them for a week or so, depending on how long it took to get to Kigali. From there, we would either go back to Uganda and fly to Burundi, or, if the war situation permitted, we would drive through RPF-held territory to Burundi. Rizu would go ahead of us to Burundi to set up contacts in the government-held section of Rwanda, so that we could start operating almost as soon as we arrived in Burundi — whichever way we got there.

At breakfast the next morning, the garden of the hotel is filled with colour and an almost riotous array of bird calls. Rizu introduces us to Iruga, a Kenyan journalist who has studied the situation in Rwanda for some years. Over fresh fruit and strong Kenyan tea, we are given some general background information on this wave of killings that has stunned the world. The information from the photographers last night was vivid and useful, but this is the first time that we begin to get some idea of the causes of the tragedy.

'The RPF,' he tells us, 'was never based in Rwanda. It was formed outside of the country, by refugees living in Uganda. That's part of the problem in that the Hutu-controlled government was always able to claim that they were invaders. The government set up the *interahamwe* — the militias — claiming that they were a civilian defence against the invading RPF. In fact, the main function of the *interahamwe* was to safeguard the government's power internally. The killings were mostly carried out by the *interahamwe,* and certainly one of the main reasons for the massacres was an attempt by the government to hang onto power.

'One thing you must remember is that there were hit lists drawn up before the massacres began, and there were many Hutu politicians — opponents of the government — on the hit lists. They were killed too. The killing, at least in the beginning, was politically motivated.'

But can mere politics explain the extent of the killing?
Iruga shakes his head. 'No,' he says, 'that I cannot explain.'

The snow-capped peak of Mount Kilimanjaro is visible
through the porthole as we take off from Nairobi on the
flight to Entebbe, Uganda. On my lap are a pile of
photocopies of magazine and newspaper articles — background reading. It is not our job to simply report on the latest
tragedies, on the most recent atrocity. We are going to
Rwanda to try and get to the heart of the matter, to try and
find what it is that has caused such killings on such a massive
scale. As I begin to read and sift through the background
material that we have brought, some of it starts to make sense.
Or, at least, I begin slowly to make some order out of the
chaos of impressions and images that I have absorbed willy-
nilly over the last few days.

To begin to understand what has happened in Rwanda...
perhaps I should say, to begin to grasp intellectualy what has
happened in Rwanda, one has to start with history. For it is
here that one sees the choices made by politicians to lead
their people down one path or another, and the consequences
of these choices.

The generally accepted version of Rwanda's history is that
around 1000 AD migrating Hutu tribespeople started moving
into Rwanda and neighbouring Burundi, displacing the Twa
pygmies who had historically occupied the area. The Hutu
were farmers and cultivators who tilled the land. From the
early 1400s the pastoralist, cattle-owning Tutsi started moving
into the area. Although historical evidence seems to point to
the two groups living reasonably peacefully together, a brutal
feudal system was forced on the majority Hutu in which the
Tutsi *mwami* (king) had absolute power, and was able to
compel the Hutu to work for Tutsi overlords. This system had
been in place for centuries by the time the Belgian colonists
took over from the brief German occupation of the territory
after World War I. The Belgians exploited the historical
difference between the two groups, ruling through the Tutsi
mwami and his lords.

It is in the end of the Belgian period that one first finds the roots of today's horror. In 1959, Mwami Matara III died and several Hutu leaders were murdered by a monarchist Tutsi clan seeking to dominate Rwanda. This sparked off a massive Hutu uprising, the first such resistance in modern times. 100 000 Tutsis were killed and many fled to Uganda and other neighbouring countries.

It was at this point that the Belgians switched their support from the increasingly nationalistic, anti-Belgian Tutsi establishment to the mass-based Hutu politicians, hoping to stave off the Tutsi-inspired moves towards independence by eliciting the support of the majority Hutus. Of course, it didn't work, but it was an important factor in flip-flopping the status quo when, at independence in 1962, the Hutu majority took political power under the leadership of Gregoire Kayibanda.

The Tutsi monarchy was abolished, and, the once dominant Tutsi became a politically impotent minority who were then discriminated against. In the early 1960s, militant Tutsis began to wage an armed struggle to regain power from the new Hutu state. After a particularly successful invasion, in which the rebels were finally repulsed only twenty kilometres from the capital, Kigali, a wave of revenge killings was unleashed against thousands of innocent Tutsis, causing more of the survivors to flee, and smashing any hopes of returning Tutsis to power in Rwanda. It was this generation of refugees which would later form the nucleus of the RPF based in Uganda.

In 1973 Kayibanda was ousted by the army commander Major General Juvenal Habyarimana. He ruled Rwanda with an iron fist and an increasingly corrupt Hutu elite until his plane was shot down on April 6 1994, and the killings began again...

The history, the geography, the psychology, and the sheer scale of the butchery — at what point do they intersect? Nobody knows exactly how many people have been killed in this tiny country in the past few months, perhaps it is half a million, perhaps more, most of them slaughtered at close quarters, most of them killed by people they knew.

This is a story of Africa, but it is not only an African story. Nazi Germany, Cambodia, El Salvador, Bosnia — genocide is a universal feature of our century. There is something fundamental to be learned about the human condition here in Rwanda. If one believes that we humans are, as individuals, each responsible for our own actions and for the choices we make, we must then ask the question: What is it that makes someone choose to pick up a machete and slice into the skull of a baby? How is this brutality made possible?

It is all too much to try and comprehend at one sitting. We will have to try to learn as we go, uncovering the horror, layer by layer. Our physical journey into the interior of the country will, we hope, also be a journey into the depths of the Rwandan psyche. This is, ultimately, what our film will be about. And the past will, to some extent, be revealed by what is communicated to us in the present.

KAMPALA

The control tower at Entebbe airport is pockmarked with bullet holes, the scars of Uganda's own past battles: the hijacking of Air France flight 139, the Tanzanian invasion and the bloody fight to depose the cannibal Amin, the civil war that deposed Obote and replaced him with the incumbent president Yoweri Museveni.

Inside, the arrivals hall is clean and spacious. There are a few soldiers in neatly pressed uniforms with AK-47s slung over their shoulders watching over things.

Glenn and I, with South African passports, need visas as do the Canadians, Germans and Americans on our flight. We stand in line outside the immigration officials office waiting our turn behind a Canadian man.

'How long are you staying in Uganda?' the immigration official asks the Canadian.

'I'm not sure, a couple of days, maybe.'

The official takes the Canadian's passport and stamps it. 'Three days,' he says and hands it over.

Glenn and I put our passports on the table in front of the official. It is just after the elections in South Africa and the excitement that existed there seems to have spread at least this far north. The immigration official's face lights up immediately when he sees our passports.

'And,' he asks, 'how are things in the land of miracles?'

'Pretty good.'

'And Terreblanche and his AWB? What has happened to them?'

'Their days are over. They're finished now.'

'Good! Good! And how long are you staying in Uganda?'

'Just a couple of days.'

'Well, I'm going to give you a month!' he says, banging the purple stamps into our passports.

This euphoria is in contrast to what lies ahead of us. It is as soon as you have cleared customs and immigration at Entebbe airport and start to drive along the road to Kampala that you begin to feel the physical presence of Rwanda. The sense of confusion and unreality is still with you, but here, just a few metres away from where you are driving, along the white beaches and the palm-fringed edges of Lake Victoria, the corpses of the victims of the massacres have washed up. Bobbing among the calm wavelets on the surface of the water are the bleached bodies you have seen on the TV screens back home.

The road passes through some of the most beautiful countryside in Africa. There are rich patchworks of maize, cassava and sorghum fields; in between, there are dozens of mango, avocado and banana trees interspersed with the occasional flat-topped acacia or grove of feathery papyrus. Dugout canoes are anchored on the beach, drawn up at the edge of the water, and for a moment you allow yourself to think of the romance of this lake, the fabled source of the Nile. But then it occurs to you that none of the canoes are out fishing. The driver confirms your suspicions: 'No one eats fish anymore, because of the bodies in the lake,' he tells you.

And so there it is, Rwanda's horror spreading in ever-widening circles, now growing smaller and more intense as you begin your journey towards the centre. Here is the first tangible thing that allows you to break through the protective sense of unreality that you brought with you from home. Here is the first tingling of nausea. The words of the driver are as real as the beautiful palms against the pinkness of the early evening sky on the road to Kampala. You realise that, while you have covered thousands of kilometres already in your geographical journey, your psychological odyssey has only just begun.

The atmosphere in Kampala is hot and muggy. It is the end of the rainy season and the gardens in the city's haphazard outer suburbs are filled with near-chaotic growth: vines and palms and cassava vie with each other for growing space in the tiny patches of black earth amidst the tumbledown walls and sagging huts. Nearer town, the once-orderly colonial houses are in a state of complete disrepair, the wooden walls and sash windows are rotted with moisture and age, and are grey with lack of paint. The corrugated-iron roofs are rusted and present a curious patchwork of grey, black, and red rust and decay.

The sky is blue with high wisps of cloud that start to gather together at the end of the day bringing rain in the early evening. Vultures circle overhead, and as we enter the maze of potholed streets and shattered buildings that make up downtown, a large marabou stork swoops down out of the sky and comes to roost on the concrete skeleton of a building.

The scars of war are visible everywhere here in Kampala. There are hundreds of bullet holes in the façade of the parliament building, an old colonial department store on a downtown street has been completely shattered by shell fire. The damage is years-old, but the memory is still fresh. 'The Tanzanian army did that,' our driver says, pointing at the ruined façade.

On the hills surrounding the main street is a huge, once-magnificent Hindu temple — and the simpler, but still-impressive whitewashed gurdwaras of the now almost non-existent Sikh community. Both are testimony to the large Asian community that once lived here, and whom Idi Amin drove out in a fit of racist madness. Very few have returned to live in Uganda, and the buildings remain run-down and sad.

The city is alive, though, and buzzes with hawkers selling almost anything you want. Despite the decay and the ruins of war, it is obvious that Uganda, after decades of suffering is now a country of hope. The signs of a country rebuilding itself are everywhere: the furious buying and selling in the city centre, the flimsy scaffolding around some of the buildings where some reconstruction is going on, and, most important, the relaxed atmosphere of the police and army one encounters on the streets.

KABALE

We leave Kampala in the afternoon of the following day. Our route takes us down the edge of Lake Victoria through the town of Masaka that was almost completely destroyed by the Tanzanians in 1979 and is only now just starting to recover. The countryside is green and fertile and the fields along the road are filled with crops. There are people everywhere, pushing wheelbarrows, making bricks and charcoal, herding cattle, planting maize, sugar cane, cassava, bananas. We stop at a roadside stall to buy iced Fanta and Coke, and dozens of little boys swarm around our vehicles (we have rented two, as advised, a Mercedes Gelandewagen and an Isuzu Trooper) to try and sell us roast corn or meat on a skewer.

'Where you from, mister?' about seven of them ask at once.

'South Africa,' I tell them.

'Mandela is president!' One of them shouts out.

'Yes,' I reply.

'And De Klerk?' another asks.

'He is vice-president,' I tell them.

They nod approvingly.

'What about Inkatha Buthelezi?' one of the boys, shrewder than the others, asks.

I'm not quite sure how to answer. It's all a bit complicated. But one of the other boys answers for me.

'He's prime minister.'

It is dark by the time we pull into the border town of Kabale. The night is clear and the stars overhead are bright and fill the sky. The White Horse Inn is the only decent hotel in town, but it is packed with UN workers. Their gleaming white 4x4 vehicles are parked tightly, side-by-side, like a school of fish, in the parking lot outside the main entrance. There is a good barbecue on the lawn, though, and we, and our two Ugandan drivers, Moses and Edward, take turns going to eat and keeping an eye on the equipment in our vehicles.

After eating, we go back down the hill into town and finally find a bed for the night in the 'World Neighbour's Inn'. It is clean, the beds have fresh linen and the proprietor is friendly. Pinned to the door of each room is a neatly-typed notice:

'Welcome to the World Neighbour's Inn.
1) Drunkardness will not be tolerated.
2) According to the law, the management is entitled to keep any luggage or clothing if a guest does not pay his bill.'

And, just to be certain that there are no financial misunderstandings − 'If any guest dies while staying, his heirs are liable for the bill.'

Before going to bed, we took the camera and some of the more expensive equipment out of the vehicles. While we were unpacking the car, we could see on the distant horizon sporadic flashes of bright light. It could have been lightning, but the night was clear and there was no sound of thunder. It was more likely that they were flashes from artillery and mortar fire. That morning in the hotel we read in the newspaper that the UN had been forced to stop its efforts to rescue civilians in Kigali because of the increased fighting there. It struck me suddenly how small Rwanda really is − we were still in Uganda, but Kigali, and the fighting on the front-line, was less than 100 kilometres away.

THE BORDER

We woke at dawn the next morning. There was a thick, eerie mist that covered the earth. On the road outside, people on bicycles emerged suddenly out of the mist, were visible for a brief moment, and then disappeared into the haze again. The smell of woodsmoke drifted through the moist air. A strange silence seemed to hang in the atmosphere, broken only by the creak and metallic rattle of the invisible bicycles moving up and down the road. A pair of hadedas called across to one another somewhere nearby — two or three lonely, raucous cries and then the feathery thud of their wings beating the air as they took off into the opaqueness of the fog.

Slowly, and then, very suddenly, the mist lifted. The sky was blue above us, and the early morning sun golden and a soft glowing scarlet against the pockmarked brick walls of the simple houses around us. The road, and the village surrounding it, were filled with people going about their business, travelling to work, to the market, to school. It was 6:00 a.m., but already the town had come alive.

We had breakfast, and bought petrol and diesel for our vehicles from the last petrol station before Rwanda. The border was only a few kilometres away and we set off through the valleys of beautiful terraced hillsides. The scenery reminded me of trekking in the foothills of the Himalayas in Nepal. The soil was rich and dark and glistening furrows of water meandered through the fields. Men and boys with long sticks in their hands watched over the herds of long-horned ankole cattle that wandered along the roadside. Women hoed in the fields, and planted crops; others carried huge bunches of bananas on their heads, heading for the market in the village. An old man with white hair and a still-strong body carried a stick over his shoulder that was hung with freshly caught fish that glistened silver and, quickly, as they swung behind him, bronze in the morning sunlight.

We came to the border. A sign read UNAMIR CHECK-POINT 2 — KATUNA. Three soldiers stood outside the prefabricated hut at the edge of the road. They were all officers. Two of them were with Unamir (The United Nations Assistance Mission in Rwanda) one of the UN officers was from Hungary, and the other was from Bangladesh. There was also a lieutenant from the NRA — the Ugandan army. They seemed both bored and a little nervous at the same time. After all, they were soldiers on the edge of a war zone who were powerless to do anything except wait, and if anything happened, withdraw. All three of them seemed glad to see us, and they were very friendly. Talking to them, though, I could sense the anomaly of the UN's situation in Rwanda. They were decent human beings forced, by the position they were in, by the decisions taken by their superiors, to witness a holocaust and do nothing.

They handed us our passports and press cards back, and we talked some more — of the weather, the crops, our vehicles, anything to avoid the real subject, anything to avoid translating into words the incoherence of darkness that lay in front of us.

MULINDI

From the border post we passed over into the no-man's land that lay between the two countries, over the first of many rivers that we crossed on our journey. The stream was brown and narrow and the water gurgled under the wooden bridge that we drove over. There was a bright-eyed hammerkop picking its way along the sunny bank and a pair of crows circling against the blue sky. The mountains of Rwanda were ahead of us, green in the morning sun with a patchwork of fields and small groves of bluegum trees running up and down their slopes.

A few hundred metres on was the RPF-controlled border post on the Rwandan side. The customs and immigration office had been hit by the fighting and the walls were pockmarked with bullet holes. The windows were smashed and the bars across the opening wrenched apart. Eleven RPF soldiers stood around the building. They were wearing the old East German and Yugoslavian pattern camouflage uniforms. Unlike the rifles that most African guerrilla armies I have seen carry, their AK-47s were brand-new and were in excellent condition. The RPF representative in Brussels had been told that we were coming and the officer in charge at the border post had a list of our names on a sheet of paper. They checked our passports against the list, and told us that we would have a guide to take us to the nearby tea plantation of

Mulindi where we would be briefed and could plan the rest of our journey.

A soldier climbed into the front vehicle and we set off. We had to drive on the right-hand side of the road. We were passing from the world of British influence to that of Belgium and, to a lesser extent, France — the colonial legacy today is as trivial, and as fundamental, as what side of the road you drive on.

So we switched sides, and began our journey into Rwanda itself. The first thing we noticed was the utter emptiness of the landscape. Until a few months ago, the countryside must have been teeming with people, but now there was only silence in the deep, shaded valleys. Like on the Ugandan side of the border, the soil was black and fertile, but on this side the fields were overgrown and choked with weeds. Here, on the tarmac, was an abandoned shoe; there an overturned bench, and over there an open schoolbook, its pages flapping back and forth in the wind. The houses stood empty, their doors swinging open to reveal the cool darkness within. The gardens were filled with bright tropical flowers: crimson strelitzias, purple bougainvillea, yellow arum lilies, but they, too, stood empty and untended, the neat pathways littered with the debris of fear: an overturned cooking pot, a hastily-packed suitcase suddenly dropped and the clothes scattered out behind it, evidence of people fleeing for their lives.

A single car passed us on the road, heading for Uganda, its numberplate covered over with black plastic sheeting — a pathetic, and useless, attempt to remain anonymous, to hide from the possibility of violent death. As we drove on, there were just more empty valleys and the increasing numbers of the grim, ugly dots of crows circling in the blue sky.

We came to our first RPF checkpoint — a thin eucalyptus log stretched between the backs of two rough homemade chairs. Two young soldiers with AK-47s hung loosely over their shoulders sat in the shade of a banana tree nearby. They stood up when they heard us coming. I felt a brief moment of apprehension; we had heard so much about roadblocks when we were in Nairobi, but with our uniformed RPF guide there was no problem and the boys pulled the log back and waved us through.

A short way on down the road there was a faintly prickling odour in the air — remotely sweet, some kind of stale old cinnamon perhaps. It was a bizarre, completely unfamiliar smell, that first distant hint of death. And then we passed a row of empty houses and the choking awfulness of it filled the car. A single dog ran out at the car, snarling with hunger now that he was no longer able to feed on the decomposing human offal. We drove on, leaving it scrambling after the car, barking madly at our wheels. The air cleared again. How many people had been killed in that village? Who were they? And who had killed them? None of that we would ever know, nor probably would anybody. They simply lay there, their bodies rotting in the greenness of the valley that had once been their home.

We smelt death once more on the short — perhaps eight or ten kilometre — journey from the border to Mulindi. And we would smell it often from now on. It is difficult to describe the experience of smelling the strong decaying odour of death four or five times a day, every day. The human mind switches off after excessive repetition, and after coming into contact with too much horror. Perhaps, though, it is worth the reader's while trying to remember, every now and then, that smelling death was something we experienced quite regularly during an ordinary day's events in Rwanda.

The road to Mulindi wound through a beautiful valley where the tea grew in ordered square fields crisscrossed by irrigation ditches. There was a pair of elegant crowned cranes that stood on the side of the clear running water. With the cranes and the ordered deep green rows of tea bushes, the scene reminded me briefly, and nostalgically, of an imagined ancient Japan in the days of the samurai. The last stretch of the road wound up a series of hillsides covered in eucalyptus trees. We came to a collection of old colonial buildings at the top of the hill. There were some 4x4s parked nearby and more RPF soldiers lounging in the shade of the buildings. Our guide got out and went up the hillside to the main building to call whoever was to be our escort for the rest of the journey.

While we were waiting for him to return, a pair of Australian journalists drove up the road and got out of the car. They had come from Kigali that morning and they told us that, indeed, there had been fighting in the suburbs of the city last night. The government forces were rocketing the RPF lines, behind which they had been staying. The flashes we had seen in the far distance on the horizon from inside Uganda had probably been Katushya rockets. The two Australians were on their way out of the country. They were unshaven, dirty and seemed almost unsteady on their feet. It was not that they were drunk or on drugs — although it might have appeared that way at first glance — they were simply overwhelmed by the things they had witnessed. Deeply shaken men, they spoke in short, staccato bursts, spilling out a haphazard array of images and impressions, descriptions of piles of corpses, of lines of refugees, of disease, of the fighting in Kigali. Even their uncertain movements and jerky body language told of horror and unexpressed fears. These were not greenhorn journalists either, they had both covered many other wars in other parts of the world, but they were utterly relieved to be getting out of Rwanda. The photographer tried harder to keep up the pretence of friendly Aussie hail-fellow-well-met, but the reporter looked at us through his bloodshot, exhausted eyes: 'It is worse,' he said, 'than you can ever imagine.'

BYUMBA

Our guide for the rest of our journey through RPF-controlled territory was to be Lieutenant Frank Ndore. A tall, thin man with angular features and an aristocratic face, he looked like the archetypal Tutsi (a characterisation that, as we shall see, he would probably reject out of hand). He wore a camouflage uniform that, in contrast to our increasingly scruffy appearance, was always immaculately clean and neatly pressed, a black beret pulled rakishly over his ear and a pair of imitation Ray-Ban Wayfarers. He had fled Rwanda as a very young child in 1959 and had lived in Uganda most of his life. He was extremely well-educated, speaking English, French and Kinyarwanda perfectly. He had joined the NRA and fought with them, until joining the RPF in 1990. He had been wounded in battle a number of times and had scars all over his body, including a missing thumb on his right hand, to prove it. Many of the other journalists we spoke to had problems with their RPF guides, but Frank helped us enormously. He was open and honest and, within the limits of military secrecy, answered all our questions and allowed us to film what we wanted to. Without him, we would not have learned half of what we did about Rwanda.

That afternoon, with Frank in the lead vehicle, we left Mulindi for the town of Byumba. There we were to interview a mixed group of both Hutu and Tutsi politicians. Before the massacres, all of them had been members of political parties opposed to the Habyarimana government.

We climbed up through the winding mountain roads of northern Rwanda, amazed by the country's alpine beauty, and by the utter silence of the abandoned land. Village after empty village passed by the window of our car in an endless, horrifying blur. Finally, late in the afternoon, we arrived at a village on the outskirts of Byumba. We turned off the main road and drove down a narrow dirt road bounded by a scraggly hedge on either side. At the end of the road was a small collection of simple houses overlooking a deep green valley. About six or seven cars were parked close together in the grass along the edge of the road. They were all fairly expensive cars, but not ostentatiously so: a 1980s model Mercedes, a shiny black Hyundai, a Honda ... they looked out of place in this poor rural African village. Clearly they were the city cars of what had once been the middle class of Kigali.

There was something hauntingly sad about their presence here in this village. For one thing, we knew that they had all been used to escape the killing, their owners grabbing what they could before getting on the road and fleeing while they still could, many of them leaving the bodies of slaughtered wives, husbands, children. The fresh dents and deep scratches on some of the cars were silent testimony to the fear and desperation that had followed them in their flight. One could almost imagine the breathless terror of the drivers and the occupants of the car as they manoeuvered the cars through the blood-soaked streets of the crazed city that had once been their home, the frantic scrabbling clash of gears as they realised they had turned the wrong corner and had to quickly reverse, the sweat of fear making their hands slippery as they waited, trapped amongst the vast flow of refugees on foot, hoping against hope that somehow, they would escape the roadblocks and the machetes of the *interahamwe*...

The owners of the cars were sitting in the afternoon sun, waiting for us. There were perhaps a dozen people, mostly men, sitting in a circle on kitchen chairs and a wooden bench. In the background women did washing and tended to their strangely quiet children who looked at us with deep, silent expressions on their faces. We spoke first to a man who had once been Rwanda's ambassador to Washington. 'The government,' he told us, 'planned to kill all the opposition leaders, Hutus and Tutsis. They had drawn up lists of opposition politicians, people whom they wanted elimi-nated. The Prime Minister, the Minister of Information, the Minister of Agriculture, the Minister of Labour, they were all killed the day after the plane went down. The President of the Constitutional Court was killed, the Director of the Cabinet, and many others, they were all killed. It was all planned, how else can you explain the killing of so many key people in such a short time?'

Another man, an opposition Hutu politician, told us a horrifying tale that we were to hear, repeated in different ways, time and time again in Rwanda: 'I left Kigali on Tuesday; on Wednesday evening the President's plane was shot down. The next day they began to kill the politicians and their families. That night they came to my house and when they saw that I was not at home they killed my wife and all my children...'

And another story: 'My whole family was exterminated. My wife, my three children, my father, my mother, my three brothers — they were all killed by the Presidential Guard.'

One thing emerges clearly from this tragic group of survivors who are both Hutus and Tutsis: the conflict here in Rwanda is far more than a simple tribal war, its roots are deep and complex. It is also clear that there was once a social order in Rwanda that looked beyond mere ethnic hatred. Speaking to these politicians — these shattered human beings — and hearing their stories has been a moving, even humbling experience, but unfortunately it explains very little. The question still remains, how then, especially if there was once an even moderately powerful and influential group of citizens who were not concerned with ethnic hatreds, was it possible for such genocide to take place?

We spent that night, our first in Rwanda, in Byumba itself. On the outskirts of town a group of young women RPF recruits was being taught how to march on the playground of a schoolyard. A few vehicles passed us on the road. They were former civilian vehicles that had been hastily painted with brown and green paint that had a sloppy resemblance to camouflage. One or two of the vehicles had simply been covered in a brownish-blackish mess of grease and sand. This makeshift camouflage was evidence of both the extreme rapidity of the RPF advance, and the seriousness with which they conducted their warfare. One got the impression that they were using everything at their disposal to achieve their objectives. Nothing went to waste, and, in addition, from what we had seen so far, discipline was good in the RPF.

The house we were staying in had been taken over by the RPF. It seemed to have been abandoned anyway. It was a simple house, with an asbestos roof and a narrow balcony out front, built towards the end of the Belgian colonial period. Inside what was once the living room there was a small fireplace and a rickety wooden table and chairs. The bedrooms had been ransacked, the cupboards forced open and anything of value taken. Old schoolbooks and torn magazines littered the floor, on one of the broken beds there were two ripped East German issue groundsheets jumbled up as if to make a rough pillow. The floor of the passageway was covered with spilled beans, as hard and as treacherous as marbles.

There were two pleasant surprises: the water worked, intermittently, so we could wash, and Glenn found an old electric socket and bulb that worked off our generator, so we could have light in the evening to cook and do the hundred and one things that we needed to do to view that day's footage and prepare for filming the next day.

We were like a small army on the move ourselves with all our equipment. In addition to our camera, tripod and sound gear, we had five trunks of batteries, tapes, cables, tools, medical supplies, fourteen jerrycans full of fuel, three boxes of tinned food, a television monitor, a Betacam player, the generator, five flak jackets, a primus stove, an electric element, cooking pots and various personal cases. Both vehicles were crammed to the roof with gear and packing it all in Uganda took well over an hour. Tonight was the first night that we would have to unpack it and actually use all, or at least some of it. It took probably forty minutes to unpack our gear, and boxes and trunks and jerrycans were strewn around the house in a state of chaos. Fergal offered to cook, but none of us knew how to light the primus. We managed, with David's help, to produce a firebomb of red flames and black smoke that sputtered malignantly on the concrete floor of the porch. In the end, Moses had to come to our aid with a small piece of wire that unblocked the jets and soon there was a roaring stove going that we could cook on.

Fergal opened cans of bully beef and pasta. There was even a little fresh garlic that we brought with us from Uganda. Our mood was good, and, as we sipped some of the whiskey we brought with us from Johannesburg out of the enamel mugs we bought in Nairobi, there was a slight sense of a spirit of adventure among us. We had already experienced, at a distance, some of the horror that lurked here in Rwanda, but there was also no point in dwelling on it. The RPF soldiers around us were relaxing, too, this evening. We were, in Rwandan terms, still far from the frontline, and they were happy to enjoy the fact that, for tonight, at least, they could rest.

When dinner was finally ready, there were suddenly five or six more people to feed than we had planned on. It would have been unforgivable to even think of refusing to share our food, but, at the same time, we simply had not brought enough food with us to feed that many people every night. Foolishly, it never occurred to us that we would have to feed anyone else but ourselves and Moses and Edward. Supper was very small that night, and we went to bed hungry. At that stage it was not a big deal, but we were not sure how long we will be in Rwanda, and we sensed that it could become a problem as time went on.

After dinner, we sat around the table inside the house and listened to the RPF radio on the shortwave band. At different times, it is broadcast in French, Kinyarwanda and, strangely, English. It is broadcast in English because many of the RPF soldiers are refugees from Uganda who don't speak French. Sitting there in the half-darkness of an almost empty Rwandan town I could understand why the RPF with their English radio, their Ugandan army experience, and their overwhelming numbers of Tutsi fighters might be seen by many Rwandan Hutus as an invading Tutsi army. Of course, the RPF combatants may see themselves as returning exiles, and as freedom fighters. However, the silence of the empty countryside we passed through today spoke not of the welcome of the liberator, but of the fear of the invader.

The next morning we woke early to film an old hotel that had been converted into an orphanage for children who had lost their parents in the massacres or in the war. What had been the hotel was a group of chalets nestling on a mountaintop overlooking a stunning range of mountains. Looking west, we could see for miles — we were so high that we could possibly have seen a good part of Rwanda. In front of us stretched an endless folded land, valley after valley, dark and mysterious, topped by golden peaks that, as the sun rose higher, grew green nearby and light blue and then purple on the horizon.

In the distance so much beauty, and close by, so much suffering. The children were still sleeping when we arrived, hundreds of them packed onto the concrete floors of the chalets. There was the smell of childish sweat, and urine where some of them had wet the thin blankets they were sleeping on during the night. Slowly they started to wake, and the watery sound of coughing from diseased lungs filled the air. There was no crying except, once or twice, from the very smallest babies. Mostly, the children watched us in silence as we went about our work, wondering at this new invasion into their lives.

Wandering from chalet to chalet was like entering deeper and deeper into a labyrinth of misery. Rose, the young woman who was in charge, took us through each one explaining how the orphanage worked and what problems they had. They had little food for the children, most of what they had was given them by the RPF. They had no medicines or bandages left. The Red Cross had given them some a few weeks back, but since then, nothing. The other aid agencies passed through here on their way to Kigali but so far none had stopped. It was difficult, Rose said, to persuade them to help the orphanage. 'They tell us they have more pressing needs in Kigali,' she said.

As we worked our way through the orphanage, filming, Rose would point out individual children. Some, she knew the stories of, others, neither she nor anyone else knew how they had come here. At the foot of the stairs leading up to one of the chalets, a young girl was sunk down on her heels, rocking constantly back and forth, her face turned upwards, her eyes staring at the sky. She was gone, something inside her fragile, child's mind had snapped. No one knew her story, and what she had witnessed remained locked inside her, she simply squatted there all day on the steps rocking back and forth, staring up into the sky.

We opened the door to another chalet. Here were the sickest of the young children. They were too weak to move. Rose and the other adults were doing the best they could to keep them alive, but as each day passed the odds against their surviving grew greater and greater.

There was another boy, wandering slowly through the ethereal beauty of the morning sunlight. There was a small white patch of bandage above his right eye. 'He was stabbed in the head with a spear or an iron bar,' Rose told us, 'into his brain. We know that at the least he has lost all control of his bodily functions, what other damage there is, we are not certain.' The boy stared at us for long unblinking minutes, his eyes wide and unfocused.

Many of the children had survived the massacres by hiding for days under the bodies of their parents, finally crawling out and wandering blindly down the roads of Rwanda until they had somehow found their way to this orphanage.

In a normal society we have soldiers experiencing battle fatigue and shell shock and victims of violent crime undergoing treatment for post-traumatic stress, but the total, unremitting horror that these children had experienced in the space of their short lives goes beyond therapy and psychological terminology. It is difficult to imagine how they can ever recover from what they have endured. The collective world of pain and shock that they now inhabit is substantially and, materially, different from our own.

This beautiful place then, was a boundary of a different kind that we came to on our journey. The mountains and the tarmac road were in Rwanda, but this orphanage was the frontier post of the Republic of Dementia — the murky edge of madness where the only border guards were your own sanity and the circumstances you found yourself in. It was the brink of the world that these children now lived in.

From this point on, our physical trek would not always be easily separable from our psychological journey — there would no longer be any need to imagine horrors, we would experience them, time and again, for ourselves. There would be moments when the borders between Rwanda and Dementia would shift quickly and imperceptibly, when the line that separated hallucination from reality would be blurred, and we would be left, half-drowning, in a spiritual Interzone, grasping at the flimsy edges of our own rationality. There would be times when the only understandable reality was the physical passage of both time and distance as measured out by our wristwatches and by the odometers on our vehicles.

This is not metaphor. It is an accurate description of our journey.

Before we left the orphanage, we had one question to ask. We didn't want to ask it, but the dictates of journalism demand that the facts be known. 'Are these children Hutus or Tutsis?' we asked.

Rose's eyes flashed with rage: 'How could it possibly matter?'

NYARUBUYE

Then we were on the tarmac road again, heading south for Nyarubuye. We knew what we were going to see there. In the grounds of this country church approximately 4000 people, mostly Tutsis, gathered to seek refuge from the local *interahamwe*. At Nyarubuye, the *interahamwe* attacked on April 17 and were beaten off by the refugees. They called in the army and attacked again at about 4 p.m. the next day. This time, they succeeded in easily smashing through the paltry Tutsi defence. By the time the slaughter was over, there were only a few survivors − less than a dozen − of the original 4000. The bodies of the victims were still lying where they had fallen almost six weeks after the massacre had taken place.

We had some 200 odd kilometres to travel that day before we reached Nyarubuye. We wound our way up the narrow hillside roads through plantations of eucalyptus trees and the mile upon mile of empty patchwork fields. At every turn in the road, crows circled in the sky overhead. There were no other cars on the road. We travelled through a wasteland where there was just the occasional squawk of a crow and, when we stopped the cars to give the drivers a rest and to smoke, the gentle sound of the wind in the eucalyptus trees.

In the car, we asked Frank about Rwanda, and the problems there as he saw them.

'Rwanda,' he told us, 'historically has had eighteen clans consisting of both Hutu and Tutsi, except for one clan − the royal clan which was made up of only Tutsis. People could move from Hutu to Tutsi by improving their economic situation and vice versa. It was the Germans who identified one *class*, the Tutsi, as a ruling *tribe*. There was an underlying racism in the system right from the start. The Germans could not accept that the Tutsis, whom they found were extremely sophisticated, and also had finer features than the Hutu, were

African. They tried to construct theories that the Tutsis originally came from the middle East, nearer to Europe. It helped them justify their policy of indirect rule.

'When the Belgians came they continued this policy of indirect rule. In fact, they increased tension by using only Tutsi overlords, and the local Hutus increasingly blamed the Tutsis, not the Belgians, for the oppression that they experienced. The Belgians introduced an artificial identity system to define the difference between Hutu and Tutsi, because they couldn't do it any other way. About the 1940s the Belgians introduced a system where anyone who owned more than ten head of cattle was classified as Tutsi and anyone who owned less than ten head of cattle was classified as Hutu. Tutsis generally are regarded as taller than Hutus, so height was another factor they considered in their classification system. They only educated those people whom they classified as Tutsis, so, for example, people shorter than a certain height were not allowed to be educated. By the time the 1950s arrived, people in Rwanda had to carry identity cards stating whether they were Hutu or Tutsi.

'Then, in the 1950s, the winds of change started to blow through Africa. Basically a feudal system still existed in Rwanda, but the king then, Matara, who was very pro-independence, tried to institute some changes. He said that any chief who owned more than forty head of cattle and who ruled over more than fifteen people had to give three-quarters of his land and cattle to his subjects and keep only a quarter for himself.

'These attempts at social change and the increasing pro-independence ideas of the Tutsi intellectuals made the Belgians nervous, and they started grooming the small Hutu elite as opponents to King Matara. In 1959, when Matara died, the revolution was started by Hutus seeking to form a Hutu republic free of Tutsi domination.'

Which, ultimately, in 1962 they achieved, and it lasted from then until the present-day chaos. Frank was typical of everyone we met in the RPF, certainly in leadership positions. He refused to see Rwanda's conflict in ethnic terms.

'How do you define ethnicity?' he asked us. 'Surely a different language must be one of the most essential criteria? Hutus and Tutsis speak the same language, Kinyarwanda. They have the same religion, the same customs. They live in the same villages. Our problem in Rwanda is not ethnic: it is political.'

That may be so, but has it not, now, in the aftermath of such an obvious attempt to exterminate the Tutsis, become ethnic?

'It will take a long time to solve this,' he admitted. 'A lot of non-segregation, and a lot of tolerance. It takes time to persuade the local people of this, successive governments have had a long time to persuade them that they are different people. And when massacres like this happen, it reinforces that belief.'

It was late in the afternoon, near sunset, by the time we arrived at the narrow dirt road that led off the tarmac into the bush. No one among us spoke much as the cars lurched and bumped along the rough road. Branches from the overhanging trees whipped at the windscreen, and the elephant grass on the side of the track was higher than the roof of our 4x4s. At the crest of a hill, we came across an open space of sudden African beauty with the gnarled trunks of flat-topped acacia trees silhouetted against the golden sky, and then the road dipped back into the lengthening shadows of the valley beneath us. We drove on in silence through the gathering dusk, our hearts beginning to pound, and our palms sweaty. There was a thicket of trees ahead of us and a glimpse of a red brick church through the leaves. We rounded a bend and the church was in front of us.

We got out of the cars. There was the smell of death all around us and the sound of flies buzzing in the air. We tied the handkerchiefs we had brought around our mouths and noses. We took the camera and sound gear out of the car, and began to walk towards the buildings. And so we crossed again into the Interzone; deep into the heartland of madness.

On the church steps was a single body, now hardly more than a pile of bones and desiccated flesh, its legs and arms stretched out wide across the steps — a rotting crucifix of pain.

I looked down. At my feet was the skeleton of a baby. Its head was smashed with a club and the shards of its fragile white skull lay on the ground like eggshells. We walked on, trying not to step on the human remains. At the side of the church were a dozen bodies — shot, hacked, stabbed. The skull of one young girl who had been wearing a pink polka dot dress showed no damage but the thin clean line of a single machete blow. Maggots had eaten the flesh off her face and left the bone clean and white already. There was a door into the churchyard and along the path through the church garden bodies were strewn everywhere, twisted and smashed, frozen in the moment of terror and death. The smell was overpoweringly awful. It hung in the air, clinging to my clothes, burrowing deep into my sinuses and cleaving to the inside of my mouth until it seemed to burn in my very brain — the mustard gas of evil.

Treading around rotting human remains every step of the path, we came to a tiny cloistered corner of the churchyard. In the shelter of a pair of brick archways the decaying bodies were piled endlessly on top of one another. The gutters were filled with blood and human fluids now green with putrefaction. The buzzing sound of flies feeding on the disintegrating flesh filled the air. It is impossible to know how many people were killed here in this corner, but it must have been well over one thousand. From the eyewitness accounts of the handful of survivors, one can try to imagine how these people were herded into a corner knowing what was going to happen to them. One can try to hear the screams of terror. The huge, earth-rocking thud of handgrenades in an enclosed space; the shattering crack of R1 and R4 and AK-47 rifles at point-blank range. The awful shrieks of pain.

And then, the slow methodical going through of the survivors — finishing them off with clubs and pangas. Those who had money begging to be shot instead, offering to pay everything they had for the privilege of dying quickly. All around this place where we stood, the pitiless smashing and hewing of the heads and throats of living human beings continued until, literally, a pool of blood rose up and splashed high against the wooden doors and stained the soft brick walls knee-deep.

Night had fallen and it was too dark to film. Half-stunned with horror, we made our way back to the cars. Moses and Edward had stayed behind while we went ahead to work.

'Welcome back,' Moses said, looking at us in the pool of light created by the headlamps. Welcome back. I have seldom been so grateful for the simple words of another human being as I was for those of Moses at that moment, and yet the horror was still with us, and would be for a long time.

We climbed into the vehicles and started back along the narrow forest road. In the silence and starlit darkness of the bumping car, the questions started to form in our minds. Who were the people who had done this? And why had they chosen to act with such limitless cruelty? There were no answers. We were left, each one alone, to confront the memory of the stench and the maggots and the howling silence of what they had left behind, to try to make some sense of it.

On the tarmac road, suddenly in the beam of our headlights, we came across a small group of Tutsi refugees who had been hiding in the bush for weeks. They were a terrified, huddling group of people pushing bicycles and carrying what few possessions they had tied up in bundles in sacks and cloths on their heads. The three or four men in the group were armed with pathetic weapons: bows and arrows, rickety spears, rusty machetes. The women and children had no weapons at all.

In the bright glare of our camera light we interviewed them. Their faces were gaunt and lined with hunger and mistrust. They were anxious to be gone, to move further along the road to somewhere, anywhere that they thought they might be safe.

They disappeared into the darkness ahead of us, and, watching them, I realised that night brought a new dimension to the geography of this ghastly netherworld that Rwanda had become. In the day, the land was empty, the valleys and hillsides silent, but with the coming of darkness who knew exactly what happened? It seemed certain, not only from the testimony of these refugees, that groups of *interahamwe* slipped across the border from Tanzania, and continued killing Tutsis wherever they found them. And the Tutsis themselves? And the RPF, what did they do at night? There were many confirmed reports of RPF atrocities, and only a fool could have believed that, after witnessing what happened at places like Nyarubuye there would be no desire for revenge.

At the very least, night was the time that the refugees from both sides would move. I wondered how many other anxious bands of fugitives were on the move that night, crisscrossing this land of mountains and deep valleys that lay humped and silent under the cover of darkness.

That night we made camp in the abandoned Hutu government administration building nearby. None of us slept well on the hard concrete floor of what had once been the office of some government official. We all drank a lot of whiskey, but it did not help. The images of what we had seen at Nyarubuye were swirling through all our heads, preventing us from sleeping. Only a few hours before, at the church, we had stood at what Conrad described as 'the threshold of the invisible'. The horror of what we had seen had left us in a strange and spiritually damaging limbo. We were unable to step beyond the threshold and enter into the darkness of evil, and yet, we were equally unable to return to the world as it once had been for us.

It had happened with surprising rapidity, within one day, from the orphanage to Nyarubuye, our parallel journeys had intersected and merged into one another. Perhaps we would be able to keep the history separate, that, at least, was an intellectual exercise — the writing down of facts and opinions in a notebook and recording them on video tape. But the physical and psychological journeys had become inseparable. The fear of moving forward and encountering yet more horror would now be something we would feel constantly. It would wax and wane, depending on the situation we found ourselves in, and sometimes the tension and the sense of spiritual exhaustion would be more intense than at others, but they would both always be there with us.

The film that would help the outside world to understand the events in Rwanda was, certainly, our purpose in being here and it was also our reason for journeying on. But, in making the film, we had seen Nyarubuye; and, from now on, the greatest challenge would not be to explain this horror to other people, but to try and understand it for ourselves.

RUSUMO

The offices of the Commune Rusumo were on a slight hill that looked down onto the road below. The slope beneath us was filled with Tutsi refugees living in makeshift shelters of dried eucalyptus branches. Smoke from their cooking fires filled the morning air with a blue haze. At the side of the administration building, there was the rhythmic, and suddenly erratic, chuk, chuk, chuk, chuk-chuk-chuk of a woman chopping firewood.

Inside the building itself, the rooms were filled with the chaotic detritus of war: shiny autoclaves and medical supplies were crammed into the corners of one room, together with hundreds of new sealed hypodermic needles and packs of condoms — part of an anti-AIDS campaign in the local district. A torn, dirty Rwandan flag lay crumpled on the dusty floor of the next room, and, in the room after that, rows upon rows of wooden boxes containing copies of the identity documents of the inhabitants of the area. The boxes had been marked in untidy handwriting with a black felt pen with the names of the villages and communes to which the people had belonged. Three or four of the boxes were marked 'Nyarubuye'. We pulled one out to take a look. The identity documents were mostly quite old and yellowed from the effects of the heat and humidity. We took a sheaf of them out to have a look. There was the photograph of the person — a blurred black and white snapshot; his or her name; date of birth; place of birth; and then, with the sudden chill of seeing the documentary evidence of historical evil, the word *ethnie*. And after it, printed in lower case letters, three simple words: *Hutu, Tutsi, Twa*. The two inapplicable words were crossed out, leaving the owner's ethnic identity clear for anyone who wanted to see. It was like seeing the faded pictures from Nazi Germany with the Jews wearing the yellow star, or seeing a wrinkled old *dompas* from the days of apartheid. All of Rwanda's hell was contained in those three simple words.

We had stumbled, inadvertently, on something that would begin to help us understand the enormity of what has happened here in Rwanda. Here, in this dusty room filled with the smell of musty paper was a clue to both the methods and the motive of the murderers.

Their methods were obvious: anyone who wanted to could find out, from this very office where we were now standing, the ethnic identity of anyone in this area — those who planned the massacre at Nyarubuye needed only to come here and see for themselves who in the area was classified 'Hutu' and who was 'Tutsi'...

In addition, everyone in the country had to carry these identity documents. Those people who did escape first the denounciation of their neighbours and then the handgrenades and the machetes had to produce their identity cards when they came to the roadblocks manned by the *interahamwe*. Those whose cards identified them as Tutsi were executed, those who carried no cards were also destroyed. These identity cards made the weeding out and the extermination of Tutsis and Hutu opponents of the government horrifyingly simple.

The motive was more complex to understand, and it led only to seeing a part of the puzzle. In finding a rationale for such extreme butchery as we had witnessed at Nyarubuye, we would still have to dig much deeper, but, at last, we had a start of sorts, we could begin to understand something of how it was possible for such evil to have been unleashed in the hills and valleys of this beautiful country.

In piecing this part of the puzzle together we would have to start with the Belgians. As Frank had said, it was they who had started this system of classifying people according to ethnicity and forcing them to carry identity documents. Their classifications were based on racist stereotypes that were not only humiliating in the extreme, but also ludicrous — classifying people as Hutu or Tutsi because of their height or their facial features, or because of how many cattle they owned. Their system had within it all the worst lunacies of apartheid. The Belgians deliberately created their own heart of darkness here within this tiny slice of Africa, and they did so in order to suit their own purposes of divide and rule in order to better exploit the people and the land they found here.

This is the way that people like Frank and Rose would describe the political roots of the conflict in their country. And they are correct, in so far as it goes. I also have no doubt about their sincerity in refusing to see the Rwandan conflict in narrow ethnic terms.

But the hard question, the question that has to be asked is that after independence why did the Hutu-dominated regimes *continue* this system of ethnic classification?

Part of the answer must surely be that the split between Hutu and Tutsi, as artificial as it was, was an integral part of Rwandan culture. The historical records show that it existed — for the benefit of the Tutsis — before the Germans and the Belgians arrived. One of the oldest legends in Rwanda talks about 'the children of Gihanga' in which the clever younger son, Gatutsi, goes to learn the secret of the seasons from Kibariro (the cultivator) while the older son, the careless Gahutu, gets drunk and forgets his task. Clearly, this is a myth invented by Tutsi overlords and taught to generations of Rwandan children in order to justify Tutsi dominance over Hutus.

Surely another, equally important, part of the answer is that, after independence with the reversed positions of Hutu and Tutsi in Rwanda, it then became to the advantage of Hutu politicians to maintain this split? By doing so, they could keep their support base clear and unambiguously the majority. They could always represent themselves as protecting the interests of the Hutu masses against the old Tutsi aristocracy.

There was another reason, too: whenever these politicians found their fortunes waning, the economy sinking, the corruption rising they could always deflect the anger of the people against them by fanning the flames of ethnic antagonism and blaming the Tutsis for Rwanda's problems.

BENACCO

We filmed the boxes and the identity documents in the offices and then set off for the Tanzanian border at Rusumo Falls heading for the vast refugee camp at Benacco, inside Tanzania. It was late in the morning by the time we got on the road, and the sun was high above us, leaving a hot, bright shimmer on the tarmac, and turning the green of the banana and coffee trees pale in the heat. We drove in silence mostly, Fergal and David in the front vehicle with Edward; Glenn, Moses and me in the rear. We were exhausted from lack of sleep, and in the car we drifted asleep and then awake again as the images and thoughts of the last twenty-four hours rushed through our heads.

The corpse of a young boy, perhaps eleven or twelve years old, wearing an imitation American football jersey that had the number 13 written on it in bold white lettering. He was lying on the pathway, his head facing away from the killing, his arms stretched out above his head. The position that his corpse lay seemed to indicate that he had died struggling. It seemed that he had been trying either to fight in a last desperate bid to ward off the inevitable or to run, to escape the terrible carnage behind him. To do either of those things would have required enormous courage.

And if I had been there at Nyarubuye that night would I have tried to fight too? Would I have tried to run away? Would I, faced with such horror, have had the courage to act in some way, no matter how small or hopeless?

In the front seat Moses and our RPF guard, Valance, talked in low voices in Swahili as we passed through the empty villages and towns. One town we passed through had been shelled. The buildings were nothing more than piles of rubble, and the corrugated iron roofs were crumpled like pieces of paper.

The blazing sun on the tarmac; the luminous green of the banana plantations and the dark earth at the side of the road; the empty houses and the smell of death everywhere.

Then there was the schoolroom a few metres away. The wooden benches pushed all askew and smeared thickly with blood, and between them there were more corpses. Perhaps they had waited that much longer to die, crouched in terror among the wooden benches, hearing the explosions and then the screams, knowing what fate awaited them, but hiding still, hoping against hope . . .

As we drew close to the border, the rubble of war began to clutter the road more and more: smashed ammo boxes, their wooden sides torn open in haste, the cheap pine wood still fresh and white and hanging in splinters in the places where bayonets or iron poles had been used to wrench them open; abandoned shoes and army boots, cooking pots, spoons, baskets, jerrycans half-filled with water — things of value that testified to the scrabbling haste of the Hutu refugees on their way to Tanzania and their fear of the RPF.

And then, suddenly, very close to the border, a huge pile of rusty machetes, axes, and spears. Tens of thousands of weapons piled up next to the road, one on top of the other. An RPF publicity stunt, certainly, but, at the same time, there could be no doubt that many, if not most, of these weapons had been abandoned by Hutu refugees fleeing to Tanzania.

Beyond the pile of weapons lay the dirty brown rush of the Kagera River and the bridge across Rusumo Falls to Tanzania. At this point the river flows fast, a torrent of muddy swirls and broken branches. The watercourse narrows, and the current plunges rapidly through a high gorge, and then drops, twenty metres or so, into a large pool at the foot of the falls where the water spins in a huge eddy that forces the broken branches and other debris of the river into the swirling centre of the lake.

Looking down from the bridge that spans the gorge and connects Rwanda with Tanzania, we saw, splayed out on the rocks below, the first of the bodies — tailors' dummies bleached almost white, their limbs flopping in the spray of the thundering water. One of them was the bloated remains of a young child, perhaps five years old. Walking across to the other side of the bridge, we looked out over the pool at the foot of the waterfall. It was a beautiful sight, reminiscent of a Thomas Baines print of the early explorations in Africa. A fringe of papyrus reeds hung over the edge of the water, a large fan-shaped palm tree swayed in the gentle breeze, and, in the folds of the gorge as it opened out onto the pool, a dense dark green tropical rainforest grew, fed by the spray from the falls. One could imagine that, not long ago, hippos would have been lounging in the cool water at the edge of the pool and perhaps two or three elephants drinking from the water under the palm tree.

In the centre of the pool, where the motion of the current collected the debris from the falls, we counted 11 more bodies, bobbing up and down amidst the brown water and the bright green of the newly broken branches and the floating hyacinth.

The television news images come to life. Here there was horror, evident for anyone to see. But, as was so often the case in Rwanda, it was in the world of the unseen that the real heart of the matter lay. From where, far up the river, did these fresh bodies come from? Did they come, as the RPF claimed, from *interahamwe* groups that were either still hiding in Rwanda or crossing over from Tanzania at night and seeking out and killing Tutsis? Yet, the RPF had controlled the area through which this section of the Kagera flowed quite securely for some weeks now. So, were these the bodies of Hutus who were victims of the RPF, or plain, Tutsi, revenge attacks?

Whoever had killed these people had attacked them far upriver, miles from where we were now, and the killings had probably taken place at night. It was unlikely, we knew, that we would find any sort of concrete answer to our questions, but it was important to remember that these bodies were not the fatalities of war, of crossfire, or of mortar bombs and rockets. They were the victims of the deliberate slaughter of civilians. Whether they were Hutus or Tutsis, or a mix of both, we could not say, but we knew that the murderers were still at large, roaming the countryside, butchering at will.

We left Frank and Valance on the Rwandan side and crossed over to Tanzania. The countryside here was completely different to the dense, mountainous terrain of Rwanda. The road we took snaked down through wide valleys dotted with flat-topped acacias, and long elephant grass swaying in the breeze. All along the road was evidence of the recent, massive flight of the Rwandan refugees. Black patches of ash and soot where they had stopped for the night and made cooking fires were all along the edge of the road. There were makeshift shelters of the long grass cut down and strewn over the umbrella-like thorn trees, and still, here and there, were a handful of refugees trickling down the road with a dirty quarter-filled sack of grain on their heads and a few other possessions on their backs. We passed a Medicins Sans Frontières tent that had been set up a little way back from the road into which the refugees stumbled gratefully, exhausted, thirsty, many of them suffering already from diseases like cholera, typhoid, and dysentery.

We reached the edge of the main camp at Benacco just before sunset. 350 000 people had fled here. Almost overnight, what had once been a tiny Tanzanian village surrounded by virgin bushveld had become the largest city in Tanzania outside of the capital Dar Es Salaam, filled with Hutu refugees from Rwanda.

Benacco camp was Biblical in its expanse. In an ironic way, one could almost imagine that this was how it would have looked when Moses led the Jews from Egypt, except that here, in Benacco, there were no chosen people and there was no promised land. There were just rows upon rows of dirty tents, and shelters made of blue UNHCR plastic filled the low hills. We drove on, literally for miles, through the tiny alleyways of plastic and canvas. The smoke from the early evening cooking fires filled the air like fog, lengthening the sunset and making the sun hang as a blood-red orb over the camp for what seemed hours in the haze.

Huge masses of people moved back and forward through the woodsmoke, carrying firewood, selling dried fish, vegetables, grain, cooking oil. An impossibly long line of people, mostly women and children, moved up from the dam in the valley carrying plastic jerrycans of water on their heads, and an equally impossibly long line of people headed down for the water distribution point with empty jerrycans cans on their heads. It was almost overwhelming to see the constant struggle of 350 000 people for water, food, fuel that had suddenly sprung up in the bush here. The gaping maw of sheer, unadulterated human need is an awesome, frightening sight, and yet, the ironies of their position as helpless refugees and that of the aid workers helping them were also on our minds as we drove through their plastic-sheeted megalopolis.

Almost every single person in this camp was a Hutu, and the tiny number of Tutsis in the camp were living in terror. We had already heard reports of Tutsis being discovered and killed in Benacco and other camps, and we knew, too, that many — a great many — of the people living here, receiving food aid and clean water, were the same people who had carried out the massacres. In my work I have been to dozens of refugee camps all over Africa, and seen, so many times, the raw misery of war, and hunger, and disease. There was misery in Benacco, certainly, although not nearly as bad as was to come later in the war, after we had left Rwanda, in Goma in Zaire. But there was something different about the atmosphere in Benacco. From the moment we arrived, we could feel it in the suspicious glances people gave us as we drove by.

There was something unsaid that hung in the dusty, woodsmoke-filled air around us. As we drove through the gathering darkness towards the Red Cross compound where we were to spend the night, it was clear that the psychosis that had gripped Rwanda had fled here too. These people had not escaped from the hatred and the fear, they had brought it with them.

But that, in its own way, was natural. There was no reason for them to have forgotten those feelings amidst the squalor and misery that surrounded them. I found it difficult to put my finger on what, exactly, it was that bothered me so about Benacco. I knew that each one of them carried with them their own terrible memories of blood and horror. Finally, it occurred to me what it was that bothered me. It was so obvious: every adult person in that camp knew who was guilty of the massacres and who was not. That was what it was that hung in the air of Benacco: a collective, unspoken knowledge of evil.

In the morning we filmed again: the rows of tents in the early morning light, the snakes of people going to fetch water, the cooking fires. We managed to track down the mayor of the town near Nyarubuye who, we had been told, had organised the massacre at the church. With his henchmen standing around us, we interviewed him, and presented the charges levelled at him by survivors of the massacre back in Rwanda. He denied them, of course, but Fergal persisted nonetheless. In the end, it was, more than anything, his retreat into snarling denunciations of the Tutsis that made us believe he had been involved.

After interviewing the mayor we did some more filming around that camp. We came across a group of men at the edge of a row of tents sharpening machetes on a stone. They leered at us, and, when they saw the camera, started to rub the steel blades more vigorously against the stone, defiantly, arro-gantly, allowing us to think what we wanted about the shiny flash of silver in the sunlight, and the slowly sharpening edge of the blade. Behind them, the lines of people moving back and forth through the camp drifted endlessly, back and forth under the bright sun, and, somewhere in the background, a scratchy, static-filled radio burbled on and on in Kinyar-wanda...

Weeks later, during the editing back in London, a Kinyar-wanda speaker translated the words our microphones had picked up. The words the government radio had been scratchily blaring out all over Benacco camp.

'*We urge all Hutu authorities and Hutus who live in Kigali to unite with those who support the Republic and with those determined to fight the invasion of the cockroaches. They want all Hutus to be their slaves like in the old days. We are determined to win the battle.*'

And here, suddenly, is another clue to understanding the mind of the murderers. In its own way, as filled with irrational hatred as it is, it is still a glimmer of sanity on our voyage of madness. It is an understandable part of the answer to our questions, as to why Hutus in Rwanda see the solution to their problems in destroying the Tutsis. This part of the answer is an old one: propaganda — irrational, unfounded lies endlessly repeated — playing to the fears of an impoverished, humiliated people, and so allowing a political elite to cling to power. One thing has been proved about the pathology of mass murder anywhere in the world: for it to infect a whole nation, there must be propaganda. Propaganda is the carrier of the virus of genocide in just the same way as the anopheles mosquito is the carrier of malaria.

Of course, propaganda put out by a beleaguered, treacherous political elite is not nearly enough, on its own, to justify the enormity of what has happened in Rwanda. It does not explain the utterly callous and brutal choices that individual men and women have made here.

But, perhaps, what it does do is provide the observer with some glimmer of pity and understanding for the patient infected with the disease.

RWAMAGANA

The midday heat rose in wavy shimmers off the peeling corrugated iron roof of the old Belgian colonial cathedral. A pair of ravens perched on the crumbling brick spire; their pointy, large black shapes were silhouetted against the blank liquid whiteness of the noon sun. Their intermittent chorus of ugly, discordant cries echoed harshly over the hot dusty churchyard below.

An exhausted, pitiful group of refugees squatted in the little shade that the soft brown brick walls of the church provided. Spread out in front of them on torn empty grain bags was the little food they had managed to bring with them as they fled: piles of sorghum, beans, cassava roots, dry and withered in the sun — precious little food to feed the hundred or more people standing around exhausted and listless in the heat. And when it was finished, who knew what they would do?

We were stopped at a village called Rwamagana, twenty or thirty kilometres east of Kigali. All that day we had been travelling through the uncertain chaos of territory recently taken. The RPF troops in the area we had been travelling through were more suspicious and less friendly than any we had encountered so far. The RPF had driven the government troops out only days before in their rapid advance to Kigali, and the rubble of new battles lay everywhere around us. Trucks and 4x4s filled with RPF soldiers moved back and forth past us on the road. The vehicles were travelling fast, and the soldiers on them had the strangely intense and faraway, unfocused look of men on their way into battle. Armed gangs of *interahamwe* still roamed the countryside, and we could feel the tension all around us.

Perhaps it was this constant sense of strain that had led to the incident in Kabgayi a day or two before. We heard the report in the morning on the BBC, and the incident had been confirmed by an RPF spokesman. RPF troops killed the Catholic Archbishop of Kigali and twelve other priests who were being held in the town of Kabgayi. The report said that the RPF had claimed that the four soldiers had disobeyed orders to guard and protect the priests and had acted on their own in killing the priests themselves, accusing them of being involved in the massacres.

'It's awful,' Frank said to us. 'The soldiers involved escaped, but one of them was killed in a shootout with our troops when we tried to arrest them and we are looking for the others.'

We were in Rwamagana for an hour or so, interviewing a nun who had survived the massacre at Nyarubuye. We hoped she would provide further corroborating evidence of the mayor's involvement in the massacre, but she had hidden herself in a room inside the church and, although she had heard enough to give her nightmares for the rest of her life, she had not actually seen any of the perpetrators, so she could not confirm our mayor's involvement.

Just before we left Rwamagana for the last section of the road to Kigali we met Sister Marie-Anne. She was a Belgian nun who had lived in Rwanda for over forty years. Unlike most other people who could get out, she stayed behind when the slaughter began. When we met her, she was standing on the road leading to the dusty churchyard. A tiny, wrinkled woman in a clean white habit and cowl, her eyes gleamed fiercely from behind her spectacles. She spoke intensely, filled with the passion and the stern honesty of those who have experienced things that normal people have no conception of. She had nothing to hide and nothing left to fear. Her courage was more than physical, more than moral — it was existential; she had no other way, now, after what she had survived, of relating to the world around her.

Her parish had been attacked by the *interahamwe,* and she had fled together with her people to this uncertain refuge in Rwamagana. She was living with her flock still, all of them homeless, all of them refugees. Their present was defined by the tiny, dwindling stock of sorghum and cassava root drying in the sun; their future depended entirely on the fortunes of war. For now, they were safe with the RPF, but just the night before, the *interahamwe* had attacked and killed some refugees only three kilometres away.

Sister Marie-Anne had the irritable integrity of those not given to small talk and meaningless politeness. She spoke of horrors seen and of fear still waiting, of faith worn down by forty years of witnessing murder and revenge, of the endless struggle in Rwanda between good and evil, of how the killings had gone on for so long, and of how the hatred was so, so deep...

KIGALI

Kigali was almost a relief. Here there was a war going on. In Kigali there were rational, tangible fears, and they began at dawn. You woke, suddenly, heartstoppingly, to the nearby double thud, thud of outgoing mortar rounds from a hillside somewhere behind you, and then, some seconds in the darkness later, their crunching distant explosion in the valleys of the city below. It was only later, when you saw the wounded, bleeding, arms and legs crushed and shattered at the Red Cross Hospital in the centre of town, that when you woke you could see, in your mind, images of the bricks falling, the hot shrapnel flying, the smoke rising and the blood collecting in pools on the ground. Somehow, luckily, you never saw faces in your mind, you saw them only at the hospital itself.

After the mortars there was the crazy swirling whoosh of Katuysha rockets through the air above you, followed by the multiple explosions in the valleys. Then the silence again, and as the dawn light turned grey and purple and became a thin line, red as blood, on the horizon, there were the hammering bursts of heavy machine-gun fire in the distance, picking off the survivors.

As the light came up and turned golden between the trunks of the suburban trees, there was the luxuriant sound of dozens of tropical birds in the garden. The bougainvillaea was a deep crimson against the high white clouds and the new blue sky, and always, as we ate breakfast or packed the gear for a day's filming, there was the distant thud of the mortars and the rockets and the machine-gun fire in the valley below. Occasionally, but not often because the RPF was winning the battle for Kigali, there was incoming fire that landed in the suburbs nearby. Even one or two incoming shells is terrifying and disorientating. There is nothing you can do, so outwardly you keep calm and concentrate on what you were doing, but you don't know where the next one will land, and inside you worry about it all the time.

Incoming fire during the bright, active rational moments of daylight is bad enough, but incoming in the half-sleep, half-constant-nightmare of dawn in a city at war is indescribably frightening. In the half-waking darkness and the shock wave of the explosion, the windows rattle and you can imagine the damage the shards of flying glass will do to you. Your heart thuds with the massive doses of adrenalin suddenly released into your blood, and your mind races with the fear of where the next one will fall. We kept our windows open all the time, and at night the mosquitoes came in and whined above our heads and kept us awake when the shelling quietened down.

The first morning we were in Kigali, Frank took us behind the lines, away from the fighting and we filmed the damage that the taking of Kigali had wrought. The destruction of a new war was evident in the large numbers of useful things that had been discarded, like the carton of ballpoint pens spilled onto the street, or the roofing material that lay untouched on a factory floor. The war was still too close for someone to take them.

The suburbs were quiet now. We couldn't even hear the explosions at the front, there was just the trundle of wheelbarrows along the rubble-strewn streets as people moved to and fro amongst the wreckage, fetching water from the trucks that RPF brought in from the river a few miles out of town.

It was clear, though, that the suburbs had been bitterly fought over, that in many places, territory had been conceded house by house. The walls of many buildings were filled with bullet holes from heavy machine guns and gaping cavities from RPG rockets, the roofs twisted and torn open by the explosion of mortar shells, the interior walls pockmarked with shrapnel scars. Here and there, dried, almost skeletal bodies in military uniform lay forgotten under piles of rubbish inside the houses, and on the walls of some of them, huge dried bloodstains were smeared on the plaster like giant unearthly maps, each wavy brown line marking out the topography of sudden death.

In a garden only a 100 metres away from the windows we left open at night, we found the corpses of two men and a woman rotting and desiccated on the concrete floor of the patio. The bodies of the two men lay side by side and there were neat holes in the backs of their skulls where they had been shot, execution-style. The woman's arms were outstretched and there was a wedge-shaped gash in the back of her neck where she had been hacked to death. All the fingers of both hands had been chopped off below the second knuckles. I had heard of this, but not seen it before. Often, the murderers first chopped off the noses and fingers of their victims before killing them — to torture them for the crime of being born Tutsi, and of having 'straight' noses and 'long' fingers.

As we went from place to place in Kigali, the spirit world of the myriad dead crowded around us, and became as real as the world of the guns and the bombs. How much of Rwanda lay hidden, unseen, like the corpses we had only stumbled upon by chance, I didn't know, I couldn't say, but day by day, after near sleepless nights the horrors multiplied all around us so that, in the end, we walked and ate and filmed in a state of exhausted semi-delirium.

The glass on the fish tank was smeared with a dried green-brown paste. The bottom of the huge, once ostentatious, tank was filled with an inches thick layer of sticky muck, but there were no corpses of the colourful tropical fish lying mixed in with the scum — they had almost certainly been eaten by somebody. The kitchen, too, was empty of every edible thing. The silver knives, forks and expensive crockery lay untouched in the cupboards where they had been neatly packed, but the food was all gone, there was not even a grain of salt left behind.

Outside, a pair of peacocks called forlornly in the empty, luxuriant garden. Inside, the stiflingly ornate white-carpeted reception rooms on the ground floor had hardly been touched. We walked upstairs to the second, more private, living room, glass from a fallen crystal chandelier crunched underneath our hiking boots, and a pair of cabinets from China with white lacquer and gold inlay stood against the wall. Everything in this house spoke of the gilded paranoia of a man haunted by the terror of the poverty that lay just outside the breezeblock walls surrounding his property.

Further up and further in we came to the master bedroom and en suite bathroom. The floor was littered with perfume bottles, silk ties and crumpled satin sheets; beyond lay a small sitting room with deep wooden panels that formed neat, unobtrusive cabinets. One had contained video tapes and books, another a collection of hunting rifles — all looted, but with a surprising number of gleaming brass cartridges still lying all over the floor — and another cabinet concealed a tiny concrete staircase that led to the third floor.

Through the hidden door and up the stairs was the study of the owner of the house, filled with personal bric-a-brac: framed photographs, a medal in a white satin case, an ornate carved walking stick. The desk was covered in dust and broken tiles from where a stray mortar bomb had hit the roof above.

And there was more that lay beyond, a few more steps and we were led into a tiny private chapel with rows of wooden pews and hymn books neatly stacked on the shelves behind each pew. Long rays of sunlight streamed in through a small window in the back. In the front there was a beautiful carving of a black Christ bleeding from the cross. The only thing that was out of place were the handfuls of communion wafer carelessly strewn across the floor in front of the altar. Here and there, one could see where soldiers' boots had trodden on the unleavened bread and crushed it into the fibres of the thick woollen carpet.

We were at epicentre of Rwanda's holocaust — the presidential palace of President Major-General Juvenal Habyarimana, now abandoned and closely guarded by the RPF. If we looked through the chapel window into the banana fields directly outside we could see the wreckage of the Mystere-Falcon jet that had carried President Habyarimana of Rwanda and President Ntaryamira of Burundi that had been shot down and crashed, ironically, within metres of the palace on April 6, only a few weeks before.

It was here, in these very rooms, that Habyarimana played the delicate and perilous game of trying to juggle the competing demands for the formation of a power-sharing government from the invading RPF, progressively winning more and more Rwandan territory and increasingly supported by the outside world, and the murderous reluctance of the radical Hutus in his own clique to surrender any power.

It was this attempt at moderation that brought about his own death and precipitated the bloodbath. The sad irony is that the massacres came at a time when Rwanda was closer to a solution to its problems, perhaps, than at any other time in its history. A peace accord had been brokered at Arusha, in Tanzania, and there seemed every possibility of installing a power-sharing government made up of Hutus and Tutsis from different political parties.

Then the president's plane was shot down. Most analysts are convinced that the missile that brought the plane down came from the nearby barracks of the Presidential Guard. In

addition, the evidence clearly suggests that the initial
massacres were carefully planned, months in advance. Within
an hour of the plane being downed, the genocide began. The
Presidential Guard and units of *interahamwe* known as the
'Zero Network' went methodically from house to house,
killing Tutsi and Hutu opponents of the government who
were on the hit-list — the men we had met at Byumba on our
first day in Rwanda. From Kigali, the killing spread across the
country. After the initial politically motivated liquidations,
the butchery was directed almost entirely against innocent
Tutsis. The massacres were halted only by the rapid advance
of the RPF.

Lt-Col Emmanual Quist from Ghana with the UN forces in
Kigali watched helplessly from his barracks in Kigali as people
were taken away and killed: 'From our compound, I saw lines
of refugees. At a roadblock I saw them pull one man out. They
looked at his identity card and dragged him away to the side
of the road. They hacked him twice in the neck, then they
turned his body over and hacked him in the back of his head.
Then they went through his pockets. When the man who had
done the hacking was finished, he wiped the blood off his
machete on the back of his trousers and went back to the
roadblock.'

Here is something we *can* understand — the planning of the
genocide by a clique of evil men and women, their minds
poisoned by racial hatred and glutted with a desire for power.
It is no more than an intellectual understanding, certainly,
but it is something we can grasp at in our battle to
comprehend the enormity of what has taken place here.

But that the killing spread so quickly, and so easily,
engulfing the whole city within hours and the whole country
within days...

There was hard fighting that night. In the distant darkness
across the valley there was the constant sound of heavy
machine gun fire and the thud of mortars. At the house,
sitting on a dirty mattress on the floor of the living room,
there was an American correspondent slugging at a bottle of

scotch. Like all of us, he was exhausted and in a state of shock. He stared at me with drunken eyes and waved his half-empty bottle around in the semi-darkness of our unlit quarters. The whiskey slopped around inside the glass, and the neck of the bottle travelled in an uneven trajectory in the space between us. 'This place,' he kept saying over and over, like a mantra. 'This place, it's just terrible. This place...' He was rocking ever so slightly back and forth in the gloom, until, suddenly, he fell back on the mattress and passed out. His whiskey bottle standing on the floor next to him.

In the morning the firing was still continuing. We were on the RPF side and we could cross only to the other side under UN escort, to see the Red Cross hospital with the victims of the night's RPF bombardment. It was the only time we heard Frank complain about what we wanted to film. 'That fucking hospital,' he called it. He knew that there were civilians there and that it would look bad for the RPF, but he didn't stop us going.

The UN armoured car took us through the centre of town, where the bombardment was still going on. To get there we had to pass through the *interahamwe* checkpoints in the government-controlled section of town. As we passed by, we peered briefly through the tiny thick glass slits above the gun ports in the APC. The checkpoints were manned by desperate men armed with a motley array of weapons: South African-issue R4 rifles, AK-47s, machetes, pump-action shotguns. They were weary with the fighting and the bombardment and their eyes were wild and bloodshot. All around, the air was filled with sound of exploding shells and machine-gun fire tearing into the soft brickwork of the buildings. At every checkpoint there were dozens of empty bottles of Primus beer and they were swigging at others as we drove past. At one checkpoint there was a young child about seven or eight years of age, with an old .303 rifle slung over his shoulder. His bearing had the arrogance of a schoolyard bully, but his eyes were dark and his small, child's face twisted into a wizened mask of what I can only describe as perfect, unblemished hatred.

The hospital was a horrible sight — the buildings crammed with rows of mutilated victims of the war. Among the wounded Rwandan government soldiers, there were dozens of women and children, and civilian men, many with limbs missing and gaping wounds from shrapnel. The sight and smell of fresh blood was everywhere, and there were craters in the lawn and blackened holes in the walls where the hospital had taken direct hits from RPF shells. The Swiss doctors and their Rwandan assistants were working flat out to try and help those whom they could, but amid the screams of the women and children lacerated and mangled by shrapnel, fresh wounded were being brought in all the time.

They were laying them out on stretchers on the lawn; there was not enough space inside the buildings and not enough time to get to them all. The RPF barrage had eased slightly, but there were shells exploding constantly all around the immediate area surrounding the hospital grounds. Here there was a child with no legs, seeping pus into his bandages; here a soldier being carried on a stretcher, writhing and screaming in pain as so much fresh blood soaked his camouflage fatigues that they clung tight around his legs like he had been swimming in them; here a young woman whose arm had been blown off, the remains a mess of bloody meat clasped tight in the doctor's hands, the white bone sticking up out of the centre...

THE ROAD TO BURUNDI

The next morning we left Kigali. We still had 100 kilometres to travel through what would perhaps be the most dangerous section of our journey so far. It was territory that had been taken by the RPF only weeks, sometimes days, before.

We drove through the suburbs of Kigali and on to a small dirt track that was the shortest route to the Nemba border post with Burundi. By this time we were all — David, Fergal, Glenn, Edward, Moses and myself — utterly drained, both physically and spiritually. None of us had slept more than a few hours every night. We were all suffering from mosquito bites, bed bug bites, flea bites, diarrhoea, swollen glands.

Because of the numbers of people we had to feed, none of us had eaten properly for days, and now there was nothing left to eat except some rancid butter from some NATO rations that we had been given by the UN troops and half a can of olive oil.

And then there was the psychological pressure of the horrors we had seen, day after day. With all of this combined, we knew we just had to get to Burundi as quickly as possible.

Outside the suburbs, the countryside was quiet again, the wind blowing across the tops of the unharvested crops, the sun beating down on the empty fields. David and Fergal were with Moses in the front vehicle and an RPF guard who was dozing in the front seat. Glenn and I and Edward were in the rear vehicle. The road was narrow and empty and overhung in places with brush. It twisted through the deserted countryside revealing the evidence of destruction at almost every turn. Glenn and I both had an eerie feeling about this back road, but the RPF had assured us that it was safe. At one point, we rounded a bend and confronted the wreckage of three vehicles that had hit a very big landmine. There was a huge crater in the sandy surface of the road, and the vehicles — one of them a ten-ton truck — lay scattered, upside down and twisted, where they had been tossed up like toys by the power of the blast. One of them had been thrown right up onto the embankment at the side of the road.

We passed this scene of destruction as if in slow motion in some terrible 'action' movie. Glenn turned and looked at me:

'What the fuck are we doing on this road?'

'The RPF say it's safe....'

'Just drive in the tracks you see, Edward.'

Edward, too, had had enough. 'I'm trying, I'm trying!'

Fergal and David were just ahead of us, invisible around the bend in front of us. Suddenly, David came running back along the road.

'Turn around, Edward, and drive back!'

'But why?'

We could see the fear on David's face. 'JUST FUCKING TURN AROUND AND GO.'

The front vehicle appeared around the bend with Moses at the wheel. It seemed enough for Edward. With a clanking of gears and a roaring of the clutch, he turned our vehicle around and we headed back down the road as fast as we could go. There was no time to ask questions, clearly David and Fergal and Moses had seen something ahead. We just drove on in grim silence.

It was only twenty minutes later when we got back to the safety of the RPF lines in the suburbs of Kigali, that we could talk.

'It was *interahamwe*,' Fergal said. 'There were two of them, armed, and setting up an ambush on the road. When they saw us they bolted.'

They may have run away then. But around the next bend in the road?

We now had to take the longer road. There was still a possibility of reaching Burundi by nightfall — if nothing went wrong. We took the long road through, twisting through the mountains and the utterly deserted countryside. From this point on, every moment we travelled in fear, constantly anxious about what lay ahead. It was a surreal journey in which fear and hunger — real, gnawing, hallucinating hunger — supplanted the sense of horror. There was still everywhere the smell of death in the empty villages with their smashed pots in the gardens and the doors and windows hanging open on their frames. But, now, in addition to this horror, every blind turn in the road, every empty house, every overgrown field held the possibility of ambush.

Here the destruction seemed to have entered another level. Packs of snarling dogs roamed the villages and cattle ran free and wild through the banana fields, snorting in terror at the approach of our vehicles. In one village, a group of cows, a pair of filthy sheep and a large pig were running in a herd together, bleating and lowing and squealing in a terrible cacophony that seemed to speak of some insane fable in which the animals were reverting to the wild and ancient state before the coming of humankind.

We drove on and on, through the blazing heat of this bleak domain, the constant fear simmering like a diver's nitrogen under pressure in our veins, the hunger and the exhaustion and the endless destruction flickering in and out of our consciousness like an awful trance that was half-mirage, and half-real.

And then our car broke down. It was a few hours before nightfall. We somehow managed to crawl to the tiny village of Zaza where the RPF had a stronghold. There Edward and an RPF mechanic set to work to fix it, but there was also no question now of reaching Burundi that day. I can hardly remember the events of that night. Somehow, we found a room in an abandoned seminary, and in the flickering light of the single light bulb powered by the generator we tried to cook the double handful of bitter mealie-meal that was all the local people could afford to give us. We poured the rancid butter and the olive oil over each of our tiny portions to try and make it more palatable.

Outside, something, or someone, was dead. The stench wafted through the windows and doors of our room. Fergal had thought to bring sleeping pills. As tired as we were, taking them was the only way to get some sleep. The darkness was not enough to bring oblivion.

CHAPTER 9

BURUNDI – A STATE OF FEAR

KAYANZA

Rizuwanna, the Gates of Heaven! At the border post, Rizu arrived with food — sweet fresh bread rolls — two vehicles and Sakamai, a driver and a rogue, but an immensely likeable character. Fergal and David went with Rizu in her vehicle, to discuss our plans for the next stage of the journey. Glenn and I went in the other vehicle with Sakamai.

We were hardly bouncing down the road when Sakamai started: 'You want beer? I can organise. Women? I know how to get you the most beautiful women in Bujumbura, you just ask me. I'll organise it, don't worry about anything.'

It wasn't Sakamai's fault, in his own way, he was trying to take our minds off what we had seen and lived through in the last few days, but his cheerfulness fell on completely deaf ears. Glenn and I just looked at each other with blank stares.

And Burundi itself was no safe haven. The country is a mirror image of Rwanda. It has the same ethnic mix as Rwanda — the minority (15%) of the population being Tutsi with 84% being Hutu and the miniscule Twa minority. The same historical context applies with the Batutsi arriving sometime between the 15th and 16th centuries and setting up a feudal kingdom of Tutsi overlords and Hutu serfs. The independence period of the 1950s and 1960s was characterised by similar ethnic infighting as in Rwanda, the only important difference between the two countries being that, unlike in Rwanda, where the Hutu majority gained rulership of the country, in Burundi, the Tutsi minority maintained their grip on the reins of power and do so still today.

In 1988, in Burundi, there was a large massacre when Hutus in the south of the country rose up against their Tutsi overlords, and an estimated 20 000 Hutus were slaughtered by the Tutsi army.

After driving only a few kilometres into Burundi it was clear that the tensions still remained. Unlike Rwanda, there was little sign of social chaos, but the tension was everywhere. Burundi was ruled by pure terror. All along the road (of excellent construction) were roadblocks of the smartly-dressed Tutsi army and gendarmes, all of them armed with South African R1 and R4 rifles. They hardly troubled us, but every vehicle of Burundians was stopped and thoroughly searched. No car got through unsearched, the zeal and efficiency of these soldiers was absolute, there was no slacking in their methods or their attitude. One sensed not even a single shred of doubt in them about what they were doing. They were quite clear about it — they were defending their state, their privilege and even their very lives. From their point of view, one only had to look at what had happened in Rwanda for them to be completely certain that this repression was the only course of action open to them.

We drove through Kayanza. Two days before, the Tutsi army had killed 150 Hutu civilians here, and burnt their shops and homes. From a distance we could see black smoke in the air, and, as we drove through town, a number of houses and shops on the main street were still burning fiercely. No one, it seemed, dared to put the fires out. Gendarmes and soldiers patrolled the streets, their rifles at the ready.

As we drove further along the road towards Bujumbura, I couldn't help noticing the expressions of the Hutu peasants in the villages and towns along the way. They seemed familiar, these faces, bored and sullen, staring at you as you drove past, revealing no other emotion. Yet, underneath the mask, each face was coiled tight with expectation — waiting, waiting, waiting. And for what you could only guess, and you would never be right.

These were the same expressions I had seen on the youths in the townships in South Africa in the terrible days of the mid-1980s; they were the faces of revolution.

Night was falling as we crawled down the incredibly long, winding road that led down into the valley where Bujumbura nestles on the shore of Lake Tanganyika. The roadblocks were manned exclusively by the gendarmes in their weird, almost sci-fi, blue, black and grey camouflage fatigues. As it got darker, the atmosphere at the roadblocks grew more and more hostile. On approaching them, you had to open the doors immediately to turn on the inside light or they would scream at you and poke their rifles in your direction.

They slowed us down considerably, these roadblocks, and soon the deep valley was plunged into night. In places, high up on the hillsides, we could see large fires burning in the darkness. *'La guerre, la guerre,'* Sakamai said, shaking his head, no longer joking and full of his earlier bonhomie.

BUJUMBURA

A drink. A shower. A telephone call to our wives. More drink. Food. More drink. Sleep. Sleep. Sleep.

Tintin would have been at home in Bujumbura with its buildings, like the Hotel Burundi Palace, dilapidated but essentially unchanged since the 1920s and 1930s, its umbrella trees lining the broad avenues and the main street leading onto a view of magnificent cloud-covered mountain peaks. On the one hand, it was like a lost city, hardly touched by time, an Art Deco Shangri-La; on the other hand one knew that it was a city of Kafkaesque cruelty where the police and army ruled with an iron fist and people disappeared without trace. One sensed the tension everywhere: in the silent, impassive faces of the waiters at the hotel, in the arrogance of the Tutsi gendarmes, and in the barely hidden rage of the Hutu passersby who watched them as they swaggered down the street.

That night in the Hotel Source du Nil we had dinner with Kadisha, a Zairean and Abdallah, a Mauritanian. The conversation soon turned to the killings.

'The statistics say that one in every two Burundians has killed someone,' Abdallah told us. It was one of those meaningless statistics that is completely unverifiable. Abdallah readily agreed. 'But,' he said, 'the sheer numbers involved give you some idea of the scale of the killings.'

'Everybody here is filled with paranoia,' Kadisha said. 'I have friends on both sides, but whenever I try to reason with them, the one side says to me that I am taking the side of the other.'

'It is partly a question of the land,' Abdallah told us. There are 262 people per square kilometre in Rwanda.'

'They never express their true feelings, these people of the region of the *grand lac*,' Kadisha said.

Abdallah nodded his head. 'They seldom laugh or cry.'

'And they hardly ever joke...'

It was a strange conversation. It reminded me slightly of the type of dinner parties one would attend in South Africa where whites — often just as well-intentioned — would try to explain to foreigners the origins of the violence in the townships, and, at the end of them, no one was any the wiser.

CHAPTER 10

THE ROAD TO BUTARE

The next section of our journey was to be in what remained of the government-controlled area of Rwanda. Unlike in RPF territory, we would have to travel on our own without guides or military protection.

Rizu had, as far as was humanly possible, organised everything we needed. The visas, the *laissez passer*, all the things that we heard about — it seemed months ago now — on the balcony at the Norfolk Hotel in Nairobi. We had again hired two vehicles, but without drivers this time — it simply would be too dangerous to risk the life of anyone — Hutu or Tutsi — from this region by taking them into the heart of *interahamwe*-controlled Rwanda.

So much of what has happened in Rwanda (and Burundi) remained a blur of horror and dark, unfathomable motives. In this section of the journey we were going back into Rwanda to hear the other side of the story; we were going try to understand the fear and the hatred that made so many Hutus rise up and try to exterminate their Tutsi neighbours.

There were fourteen roadblocks on the road from the Burundi border to our destination, the town of Butare. At the military or police roadblocks, some form of discipline prevailed, and we had very little problem passing them once we had shown our laissez passer and passports.

It was the *interahamwe* roadblocks that were frightening. There were just a few logs scattered across the road. You would draw up slowly and stop just before the primitive barricade. Men and teenagers armed with rusty machetes and crude huge-headed clubs would come up to the car and leer in at you through the windows. Often they were drunk, or worse, and their eyes were red-lined with alcohol and marijuana and gleaming with the memory of blood and madness.

Each barricade along the road was different. Some were two or three kilometres apart, some were only 200 metres apart, and each time we had to renegotiate our passage. Here three teenagers stuck their heads in the windows of the car and demanded cigarettes and beer; here a boy about ten years old with a machete was carving a huge club out of a piece of wood with the same nonchalant air one might see a country boy somewhere else whittling a toy animal out of wood; here a man with a club in his hand and a handgrenade on his belt staggered over and wanted to know if we had guns.

Everywhere there was the unremitting low-level menace exuded by men who were armed, and many of whom had killed before. You would hand them your documents, and often, here in the countryside, they couldn't even read them. That was always the worst moment, because then your lot was totally in their hands. There was no way of appealing to the larger sense of authority handed down from above by the written word. They could decide on the basis of anything to kill you. For the few remaining Tutsis — and the many terrified Hutus — who did try to flee down this road, the fear must have been virtually indescribable. Their fate at these roadblocks was decided by the most arbitrary of guidelines: one's height, the look on one's face, the shape of one's nose or the length of one's fingers...

It was at moments like that, facing the irrational, drunken, hate-filled menace of the roadblocks, that one recalled that intermarriage between Hutu and Tutsi was common in Rwanda. When the killings began, what happened to the children of these marriages? And what happened when they faced these roadblocks?

We stopped at one village where the people were friendly because we had managed to persuade a government soldier to accompany us for part of the way. The villagers were simple, desperately poor people who had to scrabble in these overcultivated valleys for an existence. Here, seeing these poverty-stricken Hutus, the glimmer of pity that one had felt in Benacco for their vulnerability to the Rwandan government propaganda machine was strengthened. And yet, there is still the troubling question of personal choice — one must remember that their Tutsi neighbours were just as impoverished.

It was here, then, that at least part of what Abdallah had told us in Burundi was vindicated. Seeing this overcrowded land was a small revelation. Here we could see how critical the battle for the last remaining squares of arable land was in explaining the part of the origins of the massacres. With an economy largely dependent on agriculture and the highest birthrate in the world — the average Rwandan woman bears 8.6 children — and ever-diminishing patches of fertile soil, there simply was hardly any land left to live on; the country, and its people, were choking to death.

From this, one thing emerges clearly from the morass of horror and incomprehensibility that has surrounded us so far: Rwanda's ethnic bloodbath was, in part, a Malthusian apocalypse — a nightmare vision of what an overpopulated world could face.

There was no talk here, in the Hutu-controlled countryside, of 'political' problems. The equation was frighteningly simple and, in it, we heard echoes of both the modern, manipulative government radio, and of the ancient humiliations expressed by the legend of Gihanga: 'The Tutsis always want to kill Hutus and live alone in this country,' one man told us. 'We cannot allow that; we are human beings too.'

'It was after the agreement at Arusha that the Tutsis in the area became arrogant,' another man said. 'They told us, "We will come back to power again, you'll see".'

Vitaro, an intellectual from Kigali, came up to where we were doing the interviews: 'The trouble began when the Tutsis started hearing that the RPF was coming nearer, they started

becoming arrogant and aggressive. But the real problem is
that there is not enough land for everyone in Rwanda.'

There was, predictably, no one who had taken part in, or
even seen, any massacres. But Vitalo did venture a comment
when we asked him what would happen if Tutsis came
through the village now.

'This is war. They would not be well-treated.'

We left our government soldier behind at the village and
travelled the last few roadblocks to Butare on our own. We
arrived in the late afternoon, and as we drove down the main
road past the lengthening shadows that crossed the street, we
noticed that everybody turned to stare at us before
continuing along their own way.

It was in this city in 1973 that Hutu fanatics attacked Tutsis
at the National University. This led to another wave of Tutsi
refugees fleeing to Burundi, and brought the two countries to
the brink of war. It was this chaos that provided Habyarimana
with the excuse to take power in 1973, and which led,
ultimately, to the present holocaust. That evening we made
brief contact with the local prefect, Sylvain Nsabimana, and
were given a government minder, Cyprien to accompany us
the next day. Without him, of course, it would be impossible
to work.

Just before the sunset curfew, we found rooms at the Hotel
Ihuliro. The war was close — the RPF was only twenty
kilometres away according to the prefect — but it had not yet
come to Butare, so the rooms were clean and neat. The
electricity supply was erratic, but the beer was, somehow,
always cold.

There was a military roadblock right on the road in front of
the hotel and, as dusk fell, we could see men in civilian clothes
armed with machetes and soldiers with R1 rifles walking up
and down the road. Someone started a fire at the edge of the
roadblock and the men and soldiers gathered around it,
talking and laughing softly as the smoke from the fire drifted
up into the sky. Somewhere in the violet and rust of the empty
twilight that hung over the town, a single shot rang out.

Almost in answer, there was the cough and distant thud of an outgoing mortar shell. And then there was only the shrill chorus of the insects calling endlessly to one another in the darkness.

This was going to be much easier, physically, than the previous part of our journey, but mentally we were very fragile. That night, as I lay in bed, every slight sound made me start up in fright. When I did finally fall asleep, I dreamt constantly of men with machetes breaking down our door or, more strangely, of huge crocodiles hiding under the brown surface of Lake Victoria.

The others talked of similar experiences. On one level, it was an indication that we had brought our own paranoia to Butare, that, after only a few days of exposure, we had inherited part of the fear and suspicion that plagues Rwanda. And that, too, would help us in our battle to understand the killings. On the other hand, all night the watchfires of the roadblock flickered in the darkness outside our window while the men with rifles and machetes kept their fanatic, unceasing vigil.

'Absolutely.'
     The RPF spokesperson in Brussels was being interviewed on BBC radio. He was replying to the question of whether the RPF would fire on French troops if they intervened in Rwanda. In the same report it was confirmed that Gitarama, a government stronghold only fifty-five kilometres to the north of Butare, had fallen to the RPF. The government was on the run, and the RPF would be advancing from the north as well now. The noose was tightening around Butare; it would not make our job any easier.

Here we entered the world of code and obfuscation. Cyprien took us (at our request) to film the roadblocks close to town. Here the people were intellectuals. Unlike in the countryside, they all spoke fluent French and had a dozen answers for each one of our questions. What are the roadblocks for? To catch the RPF and infiltrators. What do you do when you find them? We hand them over to the authorities, of course. And if a Tutsi came through here? The answer was somehow lost in translation. It was 'infiltrators' they were looking for.

But there was suffering on this side of the madness too. 'They have killed three members of my family,' said one man, a skinny, ostensibly mild-mannered man who was a school-teacher six weeks ago, and now wore handgrenades on his belt and was the leader of one of the roadblocks.

It struck me then, suddenly — everybody we had met in Rwanda had lost someone, often more than one, in their family through murder. We all know the grief of losing relatives from sickness, perhaps, or old age. Fewer of us know the heartache and the unresolved anger of, say, losing someone in a car crash. But very few of us have experienced the devastating emotional mix of shock, guilt, anguish, rage, fear, hatred... that would all come with knowing that someone close to you had been murdered.

And imagine if you had witnessed that murder? And, even worse, if it had been carried out by someone you knew well?

The whole country of Rwanda is suffocating on this pain and this hatred. There are only two types of people living in Rwanda: killers and the families of their victims.

Towards the end of the first day, the suspicion in the town towards us was growing. We could see it in the faces of the soldiers at the roadblocks and the townspeople lounging on the side of the road with nothing to do now that the economy had collapsed with the advance of the war.

In the centre of town, there was a group of 200 refugees camped on the lawn outside the prefect's office. Initially, when we arrived, we assumed they were displaced Hutus, but, no, they were all Tutsis living there. The prefect had ordered the army to protect them from the local *interahamwe*. 'I can give them no guarantees,' Nsabimana told us, ' but they feel safer here than anywhere else. I will protect them as far as I can.'

Here, it seemed, was at least one man who had been unaffected by the corrosive atmosphere of malice: Sylvain Nsabimana, a short, unassuming man with a ready smile and clear, untroubled eyes behind his thick spectacles.

This we wanted to film, and to interview Nsabimana. This man who was able to rise above the narrow ethnic loathing we had encountered all over Rwanda. It was late in the day and the light was fading, so Glenn and I set to work filming the refugees settling themselves down for the night. Cyprien, our guide, uncomfortable all day, became visibly angry. 'Why do you always want to film the Tutsi?' he asked. 'The RPF have killed many, many people. We have a refugee camp where they will tell you stories of RPF massacres.'

'We're going to film it,' David told him. We knew, of course, that the RPF's hands were not clean in this war. We had seen it for ourselves in the bombing of civilians in Kigali, and there were isolated incidents like the killing of the priests we had heard of in Rwamagana, but Cyprien's next statement defied rationality.

'You journalists always want to film the massacres. Do you know that the massacres are of people who were killed by the RPF? They show the bodies to you journalists, and blame the Hutus.'

Curfew. We were all gathered inside one of our hotel rooms talking about the day's events. While we were filming Rizu was doing a recce, visiting a Hutu priest, another good man, who had witnessed the massacres and whom we hoped to interview. In addition, he was hiding some of the very few remaining Tutsis in the area at extreme risk to his own life.

She was telling us that the priest said there were still bodies floating in the lake near his church. That area near Butare was the seat of the ancient Rwandan kingdom, and the spilling of blood was taboo, a prohibition which still had some force in the minds of the local people so, instead, they forced many of their victims to wade into the lake and watched them until they drowned.

'When I asked him why so many people participated, he said something in Kinyarwanda which I didn't understand, but he said it translated into something like 'the word'; 'the order' was given and people complied...'

There were footsteps on the balcony outside. Fergal pulled open the door to see the man staying in the room next to us quickly walking away from the edge of his balcony, closest to our room.

We had spoken to him briefly the day before. He was an academic at the university, and one of the few people in the town who spoke good English. Had he been listening, or was it our own paranoia again?

That night we heard on the radio that a UN soldier had been killed in the suburbs of Kigali very near the road we had travelled on out of Kigali and turned back when we saw the armed men.

The tide of war was turning fast against the government and its Hutu supporters, and with it, the hostility towards us increased. When we were filming in the centre of town the next morning two men came up to us. They were intellectual types, both of them schoolteachers, smartly dressed in slacks and neatly-pressed shirts. One of them wore a handgrenade on his shiny leather belt the way a doctor in another city might wear a pager.

Their initial approach was relaxed.

'What are you doing here?'

'Filming the situation.'

'And,' a slight narrowing of the eyes, concealing the menace that lay beneath the friendly surface, 'what have you found?'

The *Ecole Sociale Karubanda* was home to some 200 Tutsi orphans who were, on Nsabimana's orders, closely guarded by soldiers of the Rwandan army. That morning, with, and only because of, Nsabimana's cooperation, a Swiss aid agency was evacuating half of them to a refugee camp in Burundi. He had also agreed that we could film the operation. We stood in the back of one of the trucks with the children as they pulled out of the school grounds. In some ways, this was the most frightening thing we had done yet in Rwanda. We had seen the madness in the eyes of the *interahamwe* at the roadblocks between Butare and the Burundi border; on the way in we had been forced to negotiate each roadblock separately, at each one the uncertainty and the anxiety had increased.

But for these children, the possibility of being hauled off the trucks and hacked to death was extremely real — it had happened before, on this same road. We had met aid workers in Bujumbura who had witnessed it happening...

Nsabimana went at the head of the convoy to negotiate a safe passage for the children, but there was always the possibility that someone at a roadblock would decide not to cooperate.

The back doors of the trucks were closed, leaving only a tiny gap for fresh air, but, which in reality allowed the diesel fumes from the exhaust to pour in. The children were all wearing name tags and sitting on the hard steel floor of the trucks, and were smiling and waving and laughing as we set off, filled with childish excitement. The older ones, twelve or thirteen years old, understood what lay ahead, and they were silent, many of them cradling smaller children in their laps. There was a child who had a hand cut off, another with wounds on the head, another with a deep disfiguring scar across his cheek and leaving a huge gash in his ear.

Each time we stopped at a roadblock, our hearts would be in our mouths. Soon the children sensed our fear, and a deep silence fell on them. There was very little crying. They simply sat in the rumbling darkness of the trucks, staring at the blank steel walls around them. Some of them pulled their shirts and jackets up around their mouths and noses to filter out the increasingly sickening smell of the diesel fumes. Others wanted to relieve themselves, but there was nothing we could do to alleviate their discomfort. Outside, the *interahamwe* stood with machetes and handgrenades and clubs. Occasionally they would peer inside the back of the trucks, but this time they let us go on, unmolested.

At the border, the children were lined up in neat rows by the Swiss aid workers, and their names were read out and checked against a list: Zacaria B-, Veneranda M-, Jules R-, Dorotie N-, Vincent N-, Damascene H-, Robert K-, Adeline K-, Prospère R-...

When all the children whose names were on the list were found to be present, they were allowed to cross the border into Burundi. They walked, slowly at first, and then, the whole group of them, speeding up rapidly as they ducked under the red and white border gate at the Rwandan frontier, and ran into the no-man's land that lay between Rwanda and Burundi where they were met by another group of aid workers, with another set of lists, another set of name tags — another generation of refugees beginning their lives outside the borders of their homeland. Watching them flee towards the tattered flag on the Burundi border post, I couldn't help thinking that one day, they too would come back, and the cycle of revenge and dispossession would begin all over again.

We went back to Butare for our last day in Rwanda. We still had to do a formal interview with Nsabimana and he suggested that we meet him at the town hall and we could do the interview in his office there.

We arrived back in Butare ahead of Nsabimana, so we parked outside the administration buildings and waited for him to arrive. While we were sitting in the car waiting for him, a man called Damien came up to the car and started chatting to us. He spoke good English: 'The problem in Rwanda is that we have two tribes here. The RPF shot down the president's plane; they thought the people hated the president, but they were wrong, we loved him. It was this that led to the killing.'

Was there killing here?

'All the Tutsis here have been killed. Any that are alive are hiding. Many of them were killed along the road as they tried to flee to Burundi. They caught them all, there are none left now. It is like this all over Rwanda, only the outside world can help.'

Did he, himself, witness any killings?

Damien smiled shyly. 'That is my friend there, across the road. I have to meet him.'

Here on the government side we saw the coming together of so many disparate strands that one only sensed on the RPF side: the humiliation, the poverty and the hunger for land, the propaganda. What was so upsetting was to see the willingness to believe the lies, to see the lack of resistance to the dogma of ethnic bitterness handed down for generations and then cynically fuelled by politicians.

Yet, there is one thing one always has to bear in mind when thinking of Rwanda and it harks back to the eerie sense of the collective knowledge of evil that one sensed in the refugee camp at Benacco. The question must be asked: how, in a practical way, did you go about resisting the evil? For how long, in these tiny, crowded villages, could you hide your Tutsi neighbours? When a crowd of bloodthirsty people — often your friends and close acquaintances — armed with dripping machetes and often backed up by gun-toting soldiers arrived at your door and insisted that you accompany them on a killing raid, what could you do, when even the slightest hint of reluctance could be (and often was) interpreted as your being a 'collaborator'? And when they threatened to kill your children, or your husband, if you did not join in, what would you do then?

It is important to remember that this town was not inhabited by monsters. These townspeople, like Damien, like the schoolteachers, like the villagers we met a day or two before, were ordinary men and women. This was the most chilling revelation of all. What has happened in Rwanda is the natural reaction of normal people anywhere who find themselves trapped in a morass of evil.

It is the reaction of a man like Nsabimana that is abnormal in this type of situation. His courage, as shown by his willingness to risk his own life, and those of his family, by standing up to the local *interahamwe* cannot be overestimated. Of course, the choice to succumb to evil, or to resist it, faces us as human beings whenever we are confronted with injustice. But when injustice reaches such proportions of horror as has happened in Rwanda, it is impossible for any of us to say what we would do until we, ourselves, are facing the same circumstances.

The truth we learned in Butare was that there are very few Nsabimanas in this world, and there is a limit to what good they can do in a situation like Rwanda. Minutes after speaking to Damien, Nsabimana himself arrived in the parking lot. He came up to us somewhat flustered and out of breath.

'I cannot do the interview,' he told us. 'I've just heard that I am to be replaced as prefect by a military officer. I have no authority to speak anymore.'

He saw the shocked expressions on our faces. He smiled reassuringly. 'I'm not surprised that this has happened. In Kigali and Gitarama the prefect was also replaced by an army officer. Don't worry. I'll be all right.'

The screws were tightening around us. After speaking to Nsabimana we went to try and get a few more shots of the Tutsi refugees still camping outside his other office. Before Glenn and I had finished taking our equipment out of the car, we were stopped by an army officer. 'We have orders that you are not allowed to film here.'

'But,' David protested, 'the prefect gave us permission to film.'

'The prefect now is an army officer.'

We drove back to the hotel. For the first time, we were stopped at a military roadblock in the centre of town that had always let us through with a friendly wave before. As the soldiers were looking us over, a man in a pick-up truck roared to a stop next to us. He leaned out the window and started screaming angrily at us in French.

After we had passed the roadblock, David translated what the man had said. 'BBC, tell the truth! Don't spread disinformation about us.'

The next morning Glenn and Rizu went to try and film the Hutu priest whom she had spoken to the other day while David and Fergal and I packed up the gear. We finished the packing and waited for them to return. An hour or so after we expected them back, just as we were starting to get worried, they finally appeared on the road in front of the hotel.

'We couldn't film anything,' they told us. It turned out that the army had visited the priest the day before, and he was now in absolute terror of his life, and didn't dare take the risk of speaking to us. It was time for us to leave Butare as well, we had definitely overstayed our welcome. We packed the cars and set off down the road to Burundi, thankful that we, at least, still had the choice and the opportunity to be able to leave. Nsabimana, the Hutu priest, and the others like them, those mostly nameless men and women who had refused to succumb to the doctrine of hate, they had no such choice; they would be staying behind in Rwanda.

Did I answer your questions? Did I answer my own questions? Do either of us know any better now what lies behind the dreadful choices that people in Rwanda have made? Can either of us say what it is that makes a person choose to pick up a machete and slice it into the skull of a baby?

There is the land; the legacy of colonialism; the grinding poverty; the generations of humiliation; the effect of propaganda; the critical, and self-serving, choices made by political leaders in the past, and again in the present; the fear that if one did not cooperate, one would be branded a collaborator. There can be no question that these are crucial elements in understanding the deep roots of genocide...

I have thought about them all, and still I find cannot broach the terrible silence that lingered in the air that night at the church at Nyarubuye.

There are days when the only answer is the one given to us by Sister Marie-Anne whom we met in Rwamagana. 'It's in their hearts,' she said. 'Nothing will change here until they change their hearts. God gave us the right to choose between good and evil. And in Rwanda they have chosen evil.'

But then there are other days, when I think of Nsabimana, and the Hutu priest in the countryside around Butare. And on those days there is a single voice — a still, small voice of calm, that comes to me out of the silence of Nyarubuye.

Perhaps it is the voice of God, I don't know. At the moment, it is little more than a whisper, hardly greater than the gentle sound of the wind that blows through the leaves of the eucalyptus trees in the haunted, empty valleys of Rwanda, but its message is clear: *there were also those who did not...*

POSTSCRIPT

A year later, I was back in Rwanda with Martin Seemungal of the CBC, Alan Little of the BBC and cameraman Richard Atkinson, to do a piece on the country one year after the genocide. This time we flew into Kigali and landed at the airport together with visting businesspeople. Our passports were stamped at the immigration counter, our health certificates checked and we went downstairs to identify our neatly laid out baggage. Just above the stairs there was a large blackened hole in the wall from an RPG and a few holes in the floor where the shrapnel had gouged out the concrete; a few of the windows were shattered, but otherwise there was no sign that only a year ago this airport had been surrounded by bitter fighting.

We took a taxi to the Milles Collines Hotel that a year before was one of the only places of refuge in Kigali for Tutsi and Hutu survivors of the genocide. Guarded by a handful of Tunisian UN troops and sane units of the Rwandan army, there had been an attempt to storm it on at least one occasion by the *interahamwe* hell-bent on shedding more Tutsi and Hutu 'collaborator' blood.

Now, the whole country had done a complete flip-flop. There was a new government, a new currency and, most importantly, a new army in charge. The Rwandan Army was made up of the former RPF rebels, and the former army troops were in exile in the camps in Zaire training to become rebels.

Driving through Kigali towards the Milles Collines was a surreal experience. The taxi took us down the road we had come in from the north those first few hours in Kigali; past the suburb where the Amahoro stadium and our safe house lay; past a half-completed building that housed an RPF machine-gun post where we had filmed; down the road where we had travelled in a sealed UN armoured vehicle, with the sound of mortars exploding nearby, and through the heavy bullet-proof glass slits, just able to get glimpses of the desperate men and boys manning the *interahamwe* road-blocks...

Everywhere now there were people moving to and fro conducting the workday business of an African capital; carrying cans of water, bags of maize, bundles of sweet potatoes on their heads; selling chickens, shampoo and pencils from tiny roadside stalls; and, all over the city, building — plastering over bullet holes, replacing shattered roofs, laying mud bricks over mortar holes in the walls. In the centre of the city there were groups of men and women clearly in government employ fixing the public buildings: replanting grass in the traffic circles, painting the post office, sweeping up spent cartridges and fragments of glass and concrete in the Ministry of Information.

Peace. I seemed to be seeing things in slow motion as we passed the scenes that had, so recently, held the spectre of such horror; and my mind was filled with uncertain emotions. How could one reconcile the terrors that had existed here only a few hundred days before with the vibrant energy displayed all around the city now? It was tempting to see this renewal as a closing of the circle of violence and the beginning of a new cycle of peace.

I wanted, needed, to see Kigali in this way, but even on the plane from Nairobi we had read the reports of arms being supplied clandestinely to the Hutu extremists in the camps in Zaire, and of secret military training sessions being held under cover of darkness when the UN personnel had left the camps. There was lots of talk of reconciliation, but the reality was that both sides were preparing themselves for another clash. It was not yet time in Rwanda to talk of permanent peace.

One late afternoon, as the light was fading, we interviewed Rakiya Omaar of the organisation, African Rights, in the garden of the Milles Collines. She spoke angrily and articulately about the ruthless efficiency with which the genocide had been carried out and the urgent need for justice if there was to be any hope for reconciliation in Rwanda.

But there was one matter I particularly wanted to ask her about. In the African Rights' book on the genocide *Rwanda: Death, Despair and Defiance* there is a chapter entitled 'The Killers and their Accomplices' in which they list a large number of people whom they claim were directly implicated in either the killing or in the planning of the massacres. On page 116 it reads:

'Prefecture of Butare

* Sylvain Nsabimana, préfet. He replaced Jean Baptiste Habyarimana who was removed on 19 April because of his refusal to implement the interim government's campaign of murder. The killings began in Butare the day Nsabimana took the reigns of power.'

'Yes,' Rakiya told me. 'The BBC got it all wrong in their film. I found out that Nsabimana wasn't such a nice person after all.'

'I worked on that film,' I said hesitantly.

'Oh really? Well, I have to tell you, you got Nsabimana very wrong.'

But there were rumours that he was suing her for defamation?

'He's suing me from where he is in Nairobi. Let him, I don't care.'

There was, though, no doubt that when we arrived in Butare he was protecting a number of Tutsis and that he definitely arranged for those Tutsi orphans to be evacuated, I told her.

'Yes,' she said. 'There is no doubt that he saved people, but he also killed.' She hesitated for a moment. 'It's just one more example of how incredibly complex the situation in Rwanda is.'

Judgement will be passed on those who were responsible for the genocide in Rwanda. Whether Nsabimana is guilty remains to be seen. The reality is, that given the country's almost total lack of judicial resources and the limited aid the rest of the world is giving to Rwanda, we may never know the complete truth about what happened.

But, even so, there remains still the one central issue:

What would you, or I, have done in the same situation? In that simple question is contained the entire meaning of everything that has taken place there.